Reacting to the
Spending Spree

POLICY CHANGES WE *CAN* AFFORD

D1367654

The Hoover Institution gratefully acknowledges
the following individuals and foundations
for their significant support of the

*John and Jean De Nault Task Force on
Property Rights, Freedom, and Prosperity*

JOHN AND JEAN DE NAULT

THE JM FOUNDATION

HOOVER INSTITUTION TASK FORCE ON PROPERTY RIGHTS, FREEDOM, AND PROSPERITY

Reacting to the
Spending Spree
POLICY CHANGES WE *CAN* AFFORD

EDITORS
Terry L. Anderson
Richard Sousa

CONTRIBUTORS
Terry L. Anderson
Jagdish Bhagwati
Charles W. Calomiris
Richard A. Epstein
Stephen H. Haber
Kevin A. Hassett
James L. Huffman
F. Scott Kieff
Gary D. Libecap
Henry E. Smith

HOOVER INSTITUTION PRESS
Stanford University, Stanford, California

The Hoover Institution on War, Revolution and Peace, founded
at Stanford University in 1919 by Herbert Hoover, who went on
to become the thirty-first president of the United States, is an
interdisciplinary research center for advanced study on domestic
and international affairs. The views expressed in its publications are
entirely those of the authors and do not necessarily reflect the views
of the staff, officers, or Board of Overseers of the Hoover Institution.

www.hoover.org

Hoover Institution Press Publication No. 575

Hoover Institution at Leland Stanford Junior University,
Stanford, California, 94305-6010

First printing 2009
16   15   14   13   12   11   10   09   9   8   7   6   5   4   3   2   1

Manufactured in the United States of America

The paper used in this publication meets the minimum
Requirements of the American National Standard for
Information Sciences—Permanence of Paper for Printed
Library Materials, ANSI/NISO Z39.48-1992.⊗

Library of Congress Cataloging-in-Publication Data
Reacting to the spending spree : policy changes we can afford /
edited by Terry L. Anderson and Richard Sousa.
   p.   cm.
Includes bibliographical references and index.
ISBN 978-0-8179-3002-8 (pbk. : alk. paper)
1. Fiscal policy—United States.   2. Financial crises—
United States—History—21st century.
I. Anderson, Terry Lee, 1946–   II. Sousa, Richard, 1949–
HJ275.R27   2009
336.73—dc22   2009019783

Contents

Introduction

Terry L. Anderson and **Richard Sousa**

D uring the grueling campaign to win his party's nomination and the head-to-head competition with John
McCain, candidate Barack Obama brought his message of
"hope and change" to a country yearning for both. President
Obama entered the White House with a set of challenges that no
U.S. president in recent history has faced. He confronts an economic crisis of proportions unthinkable just a few short months
before, unpopular wars in Iraq and Afghanistan, diminished loyalty
among longtime international allies, the continued threat of terrorism, and a populous questioning the ability of all branches of government to govern and doubting the efficacy of markets. Add to all
of this the massive bailout and stimulus packages, a burgeoning
national debt, political partisanship at its height, climate change,
aging infrastructure, skyrocketing health-care costs, and failing
schools, and the list seems to include everything but curing the
common cold.

The question is whether the momentum of the president's campaign, election, and inauguration is enough to implement the
changes necessary to meet the hopes and expectations of the American citizens.

The president has said repeatedly that his highest priority is solving the county's economic problems—getting people back to work,

stabilizing financial markets, freeing up frozen credit markets, and, in general, rebuilding confidence in the U.S. economy. But he acknowledges that improving the economy is not the only problem. His solution to the economic crisis, and all the other problems, is a massive spending spree unprecedented in U.S. history.

Typically, little is accomplished in a presidential administration's first hundred days, but many are looking at the hundred-day mark as the first milestone for the Obama administration. The path followed since January 20 should foreshadow President Obama's direction for the rest of his presidency. That path clearly calls for a greater role for the government in the economy at the industry, firm, and individual levels.

No one would argue that the economy has not faltered, but it does not follow that the cause is the failure of the fundamental principles on which the U.S. economy is built. Those principles, which underpin our market system, are free markets, an open economy, free trade, the rule of law, and well-defined and uniformly enforced property rights.

The Hoover Institution's Task Force on Property Rights, Freedom, and Prosperity was established in late 2008 to study those principles in the context of historical and contemporary examples and to promote meaningful dialogue about their effectiveness. The task force's eleven members fully embrace the goal of examining the role of government in providing a stable legal system for protecting property rights and encouraging economic growth while promoting individual responsibility and liberty.

When the task force met in early March 2009, the magnitude of the issues facing the Obama administration was becoming increasingly clear. Because the members of the task force felt their expertise could shed light on how those issues could be handled without spilling as much governmental red ink, they decided to write this book. Eight members of the task force (three could not participate due to other commitments) and two outside experts wrote chapters analyzing the Obama administration's approach to a wide range of public policies.

To be clear, this is not a book solely about the first hundred days of the Obama presidency; it is a book about how a stable rule of law, secure property rights, and an open economy provide the foundation on which the administration can build more effective policies in the next 1,300 days. The consistent theme of this book is that we should not abandon the principles that have served us so well throughout our history. We should not make decisions now, based on the political expediency of action, polling, and special-interest pressures, that will have long-run ill effects—whether anticipated or not.

From the name of the task force one can correctly infer that it is populated with economists and legal experts who study the evolution of property rights, their protection, and their importance to economic growth. This team of scholars tackled a subset of policy issues to which their expertise applied; doing more would have required a much larger team and would have resulted in a longer, inaccessible tome. The intent of the coverage here is to provide a lens through which other policy issues can be examined. Some chapters offer prescriptions to President Obama and suggest specific solutions to the problems his administration is facing. Others are more general and wide sweeping, offering counsel based on sound economic principles and clear-thinking incentive schemes.

The policy analyses and recommendations in this book are not meant to criticize without being constructive, but are meant to offer alternative approaches and guidance on how to avoid pitfalls. Because the economy has received so much attention from the Obama administration, the lead chapters examine the incentives, good and bad, found in the proposed financial fixes. The first three chapters suggest regulatory reforms for the banking sector and analyze President Obama's tax policies. The chapters that follow analyze narrower policy issues—patents, global warming, green jobs, labor, health care, and infrastructure investment. The book concludes with a discussion of the important interface between the Obama administration's policies and the global economy, especially as those policies may discourage trade and growth through protectionism. That chapter appropriately asks whether President Obama's leadership and charisma can prevent the United States from following a path of protectionism that will not only harm the U.S. economy but slow the world's path to economic recovery.

The Hoover Institution Task Force on Property Rights, Freedom, and Prosperity, which was the catalyst for this project, includes Terry Anderson (Hoover Institution and PERC) and Gary Libecap (Hoover Institution and University of California, Santa Barbara) as cochairs and members Daron Acemoglu (MIT), Charles Calomiris (Columbia University), Richard Epstein (Hoover Institution and University of Chicago Law School), Stephen Haber (Hoover Institution and Stanford University), James Huffman (Lewis and Clark Law School), Scott Kieff (Hoover Institution and Washington University School of Law), Jonathan Macey (Yale Law School), James Robinson (Harvard University), and Henry Smith (Harvard Law School). The eight members who participated in this publication were joined by Jagdish Bhagwati (Nobel laureate from Columbia University) and Kevin Hassett (American Enterprise Institute).

As editors, we thank the chapter authors who met tight deadlines and responded promptly to editorial comments. In addition, we thank John Raisian, the Tad and Dianne Taube Director of the Hoover Institution; and Marshall Blanchard, Jennifer Presley, and Ann Wood of the Hoover Institution; and Mandy Scott-Bachelier of PERC for her cover design. Finally, we thank the Hoover Institution donors who have invested in this task force: Jean and John De Nault and the JM Foundation. We hope this book provides a return on their investments in the form of "ideas defining a free society."

1 Wrong Incentives from Financial System Fixes

Stephen H. Haber and F. Scott Kieff

F ew doubt the seriousness of the recent crisis afflicting the financial systems of the United States and the world. Few claim that nothing needs to be fixed. And few have missed the major debates about what types of solutions are best—often conducted at high volume, intensity, and frequency. So rather than try to add to one side or the other of the well-rehearsed arguments about each type of proposed reform, we try to refocus the analysis on some core incentives: when the basic rules of the game are changing, property rights and the rule of law are too ill-defined, creating exactly the wrong incentives for investment and economic growth. The wrong incentives created by repeated surges of bold government action pose risks that have direct, short-term impacts, which we fear have been seriously underexplored during both the end of the Bush administration and the beginning of the Obama administration. We hope that, by pointing out these risks, they can be significantly mitigated at relatively low cost.

We begin by recommending a change to the general approach: halt soon the introduction of new, bold programs. We are not saying that nothing should be done; we are saying that it is important in times like these for government to reach closure on its decisions so that it can pick one set of rules of the game and then stick to them. We then focus more narrowly on the process of structuring workouts from bad deals and recommend avoiding approaches that undermine bankruptcy. Bankruptcy allows the large group of private professionals who are experts at restructuring or winding up bad deals—consultants, financiers, lawyers, managers, and so on—to get involved. Given the magnitude of the problem of toxic assets, any solution to the current crisis will almost certainly need to involve these private actors. We then explore how particular reform proposals can be implemented without running afoul of the cautions that are the focus of our effort. In the final analysis, we applaud the Herculean efforts by so many serious thinkers in the Bush and Obama administrations and outside government who have thrown themselves into this important work in good faith and with great sacrifice. All we can hope to add to the conversation are these relatively easy-to-deploy (and important to deploy quickly) tools for mitigating some vital but underappreciated risks with proposed financial system fixes.

Reviewing Present Approaches

Four broad categories of approaches to solving the present crisis have been either tried or proposed by the administrations of both Bush and Obama, as well as by other countries facing similar problems today and in the past:

1. Let the markets and courts work it out, using institutions such as foreclosure and bankruptcy directly or as a backdrop.
2. Have the government take over the banks and nationalize them, taking control rights as well as cash flow rights. The government then cleans the balance sheets by selling off toxic assets, and re-privatizes the banks.
3. Have the government recapitalize the banks by injecting cash

in exchange for preferred shares that have cash flow rights but not formal control rights.

4. Have the government buy up the toxic assets in a special bank or institution created for that purpose, leaving control rights and cash flow rights in the hands of shareholders.

Most government rescue programs, including the one announced in March by Treasury Secretary Geithner are hybrids of at least two of these four broad strategies. While each strategy has advantages and disadvantages, the second and fourth require the government to act directly on markets as a buyer, seller, or manager of assets or firms. Strategies two, three, and four also have an indirect effect on markets in that the government is changing the underlying rules of the game by changing various laws, regulations, or norms of practice. Which solution societies arrive at depends on their political institutions. In the U.S. case, the problem facing political decision makers is as follows:

If they let the markets and courts work it out, in time banks and other financial intermediaries will foreclose on properties and those foreclosed properties will be sold on markets. The problem is that this solution involves a lot of pain for two groups: bank shareholders (who have to write down their capital) and voters (who have to sit by while they are either forced out of their houses or watch the market value of their homes plummet). Another risk is that a change in the underlying psychology of consumers will develop a logic all its own, resulting in a long-term recession much like the one Japan suffered in the 1990s. This solution is therefore not politically acceptable—at least not to a government that wants to get elected again.

The political dangers in having the government nationalize the banks (strategy two) are several. First, the government can be accused of socialism. Second, it is not clear that the government actually has the statutory authority to nationalize banks or that it can develop enough political support to make a fundamental

change in that statutory authority. Third, if the plan winds up costing taxpayers trillions of dollars, the government will be the only
one to blame.

For option three, the buying of preferred shares, there await two
horns of a dilemma. On the one side lies the appearance that the
government has simply given away too much money while failing
to take control away from those seen as having contributed to the
underlying problem. On the other sides lies the reality that the government actually is taking a great deal of control, which is one reason some banks have tried desperately to return the money they
received through the TARP program created by former Treasury
Secretary Paulson. Although the preferred stock may not convey
control rights as a formal matter, the ability to grant or withhold
future cash injections conveys a great deal of control. Control also
is wielded by the ongoing threat of shut down or other unfavorable
action in response to regulatory reviews like the stress tests, or by
the ongoing threat that any member of a bank's leadership or rank
and file can be publicly called to the carpet regarding their compensation package.

There is also a political and economic danger to solution four,
the government buying the toxic assets via an institution especially
created for that purpose. The basic problem is that the government
will inevitably pay more for the assets than their market value, for
at least two reasons. First, the owners of the assets (the banks) know
the quality of the assets better than the government. Second, the
government will have an incentive to pay a price as close to that
demanded by the bankers because, to the degree that the government pays less than the book value, it will require the banks to write
down capital, in turn leaving the banks undercapitalized when the
process is done. This may mean, in turn, that the government
would have to undertake yet another rescue plan: to recapitalize the
banks by buying more shares.

Treasury Secretary Paulson's solution was number four, which was politically viable for only three days. Treasury Secretary Geithner's plan is a combination of solutions one and four, but the government has already deployed solution three via the TARP program. The end result is a curious hybrid. The government tries to bring private market actors into the solution by giving investors the opportunity to buy toxic assets. At the same time, most of the financing for these transactions comes from the government, via an equity match from the Treasury and via a loan from the FDIC. Private actors bear some risk because they must put up part of the capital and must service a loan from the government to cover much of the rest, but they have the option of walking away from bad assets because the loans are nonrecourse (they are collateralized only by the assets being purchased). The government has also, however, taken preferred stock ownership stakes in the banks, via the TARP program.

In short, there are a lot of moving parts to the government's approach. Not only can they work at cross purposes to one another, but the high degree of ambiguity about whether the next government action will target any particular margin creates a huge disincentive among market actors to invest in any particular direction.

A related concern with this hybrid set of strategies is that they are so inherently burdened by the huge risks of the government paying either too much or too little that they lead to the government implementing its goals through a protracted series of moves. As discussed more fully below, we think that whatever benefits may come from getting the approach exactly right through careful titration are eclipsed by the risks of multiple rounds of bold actions.

The bottom line is that at least two key unintended consequences follow when market actors come to expect that the government will continue to change the institutions in an open-ended way. The first is that the belief the government will step in again in the future encourages moral hazard: private actors may take too much risk, expecting to be bailed out in a future round of government action. The second is that the belief the government will step in later may discourage private market actors from acting now, considering it prudent to wait until the government provides an even more attractive program.

We think it can be fine for the government to focus on approaches that facilitate coordination among private actors as the direct, first-order effect, so long as it avoids approaches that will require further qualitative shifts of the type that would cause overall uncertainty about what the rules of the game will be. Although the uncertainty created by successive deployment of bold moves may technically be a second-order effect in that it is indirect, it is far too big to be ignored.

The Importance of Final Moves to Stimulating Regrowth

Showing their determination to address the present crisis, President Obama, Treasury Secretary Geithner, and Federal Reserve Chairman Bernanke have each proclaimed on several occasions, including as recently as early March, that they will take whatever steps are needed to help resolve the economic crisis. The message is in part constructive in providing a calming effect on anxious people in their roles as both citizens and market actors. But the message also is in part destructive, especially against a backdrop of several months of bold moves, going back to Paulson's original plan of direct government purchase of toxic assets in that it strongly suggests that each round of moves is not the last.

This is a serious problem because when market actors think that further significant changes are coming, they find it difficult to engage in the commercial activity our economy needs for recovery. A great deal of wealth still exists throughout the economy, in the form of labor, money, tangible assets such as factories, equipment, inventory, and real estate, and intangible assets such as securities, commercial paper, skills, and intellectual property. Further economic activity requires that these wealth components be put to work: that they be exchanged with one another through new commercial activity. But many of those assets are waiting on the sidelines. Many others are tied down in existing transactions that are not doing well at the moment; but in order for them to be redeployed, their deals must be unwound.

In normal times, deals are routinely made and modified to meet the changing needs of the private actors involved in them, who are remarkably adept at integrating new information and preferences into deals when they can predict what the basic rules of the game are likely to be. But bold government actions—and the expectation of more such actions in the future—are game-changing events. Some of these changes are the direct consequence of new laws and regulations; others are a bit more subtle. When the government spends vast sums of money on emergency programs, it has a huge impact in the short run on relative costs for taking particular risks and opportunities and, in the slightly longer run, on expectations about tax rates, inflation, and the scope of government in the future. The problem is that private actors have a difficult time taking the actions we need now when they think the rules of the game—the laws, regulations, and contracting environment—are likely to change in big ways. Such a paralysis affects those holding assets that are ready to be deployed as well as those who own assets tied up in bad deals.

Consider those who are holding assets that are ready to be deployed. When facing the possibility of significant changes in tax rates, enforceability of contracts, and available subsidies that the government is presently employing and considering, every market actor risks feeling like a patsy for diving into deals too soon to successfully operate under the new rules. It might seem that the government could employ the normal tools that private actors use in deals to mitigate the anxieties of those among their counterparties who are early movers, such as committing to what deal-makers call "most favored nation clauses," and the like. When a seller uses a clause like this in a contract with a first buyer, the seller is constraining herself not to contract with any other buyer at a lower price without also giving the first buyer that same low price. But the government can't make such commitments about its present emergency financial actions for at least three reasons. First, it would be difficult to figure out what commensurabilities, if any, exist across the various programs on offer, which means it would be almost impossible to determine whether everyone were being given the same or a different deal. Second, even if the exchange rates among such programs were determined, each program would then have to be as expensive as the others, making their aggregate cost enormous. Third, it is not clear that any market actor would bank heavily on a government commitment to equal treatment, especially against the backdrop of rapidly changing behavior. After witnessing Lehman Bros. not receiving the same bailout as AIG, one would expect treatment to vary, not to hold constant.

A somewhat different set of problems faces those presently in bad deals that must get unwound. Ironically, the expectation of changes to the rules of the game causes strategic paralysis in any party who thinks she or he is suffering particular economic trauma from her present deal. In normal times, those involved in bad deals have strong reasons to cut their losses and get out. But as new bailouts, tax breaks, insurance, and other tools designed to mitigate financial trauma are rolled out, those facing such trauma have large incentives to stay in, hoping that if the mere passage of time won't bring a particular fix their way, then further trauma might.

Although all of the above argue that government leaders should wrap up their actions sooner rather than later, we recognize that there are important reasons for not doing so too soon. In some cases, leaders may have wanted more internal vetting; in others they may have wanted to test the applications of their actions; and in others they may have figured that beginning with low amounts would avoid overpayments. We are not trying to fault our leaders for taking such concerns seriously.

What we are trying to emphasize here is that political leaders must not overlook, especially now, after several rounds of action, that the benefits generated from those actions must be weighed against the too often underexplored costs of having the market think our leaders are likely to act further. Our leadership must bake into their thinking the importance of credibly committing themselves to stop making further game-changing moves and then signal that to the market so as to induce private actors to move much faster in unwinding their bad deals and in forging new ones.

Imprudently Tolling the Death of Bankruptcy

The problems of bad deals are particularly acute during difficult times like these. A great number of ongoing deals have turned out badly, as they either contributed to the downturn or were a result of it. Despite ongoing debates about the direction of causation, assigning blame may be less important to the economy as a whole than the need to simply ensure that the resources tied up in these deals are quickly put to higher and better uses. In addition, the problems of bad deals will not go away. When new ventures are launched, especially in such times of uncharted conditions, a great number will fail, and the rules of the game must be structured so as not to leave those assets sidelined and unable to contribute to economic recovery.

Now, and for the foreseeable future, our society has a particularly acute need for dealing well with failure. Professionals who are highly trained, experienced, and skilled, who are particularly adept at swooping into a failing or failed enterprise to turn things around or at least wind things up most productively would do just the trick. Specialized legal rules and organizations would provide the essential frameworks. The fortunate news is that our society has done a great job in building both the professionals themselves as well as the legal system associated with bankruptcy practice. The unfortunate news is that so many of the present approaches to emergency action may be tolling their death knell.

Like the members of any profession, those involved in turn-around and windup are good at what they do. Their practice has evolved over decades, supported by robust and diverse intellectual and academic foundations and honed by richly competitive practice.

In contrast, politicians are not experts at dealing productively with business failures. Yet many of the government actions taken to steer failing ventures away from bankruptcy have crowded out the experts our society has created to deal with such issues. Those experts make their living by acting within and against the backdrop of the bankruptcy system and thus have no reason to throw themselves into the mix when matters are being handled directly by the government (nor do they have the power to act through these governmental avenues). Some may be tempted to help, either out of altruism or in hopes of earning a share of the value they contribute to the rescue—such as taking salaries of a dollar a year with the right to a bonus if they are able to turn a profit. But they may ultimately be dissuaded by the real risk they face of being demonized by the base populism some in government and the media have recently directed toward some of those not involved in the private sector's failed decisions of the past who were asked to help save at least the non-failed components of business to prevent the public from having to take on even more risk.

At the same time, it makes little sense to favor the incumbents in the failed businesses over those who specialize in turnaround and windup. In some cases the incumbents have been poor custodians of the enterprise, leading to its failure; in some cases some aspect of the relationships among the incumbents—contractual or otherwise—was just not working well enough to prevent the business from failing. In other cases, there is no blame, but the incumbents' ability to add value to their enterprises will be much greater when their enterprise is functioning rather than failing because their skill sets are oriented for functioning enterprises. In all cases the present failure situation provides strong reasons to favor including those who are expert at the business of dealing productively with business failure.

Not only do present emergency actions risk crowding out the experts who deal most productively with business failure, but the fact that government has provided alternatives to bankruptcy significantly undermines the viability of the entire bankruptcy system. Although, like any legal system, our system of bankruptcy laws and courts is hugely imperfect, it has evolved significantly over the past century so as to be highly adept at facilitating the smooth, deliberate, and fair process of maintaining and distributing value. The vitality of our bankruptcy system facilitates entry into risky enterprises by facilitating exit, and in turn facilitates re-entry as assets are re-deployed. Bankruptcy provides all those who invest in an enterprise—labor, management, shareholders, secured creditors, general unsecured creditors, and so on—with a set of rules under which they can expect to operate when the business gets reorganized or wound up.

Extensive debates over many years have developed in the bankruptcy system a range of methods for addressing the myriad concerns facing the many constituencies. Yet no categorically new concern or constituency has been brought forth to support the present emergency alternatives to bankruptcy. This precedent means that in the future almost any argument may be used to justify such a striking derogation from established bankruptcy practice—whatever it may be at that time. In future iterations of failure (and even in its impending arrival), all savvy players should expect that, if the political will can be mustered, they may experience (by their own design or otherwise) a set of rules governing their reorganization or windup that are totally different from those of whatever bankruptcy system is then in effect. Today's examples of such justifications for veering from established rules include those businesses said to be "too big to fail" because of the ways in which they are networked with the rest of our economy and those that impact consumers who are too small to fail because they don't have enough overall wealth. Because most companies in a well-functioning economy do business with many other companies as well as with a large number of consumer purchasers, investors, borrowers, or lenders (either directly or indirectly), the precedent being set by the emergency actions makes most businesses into credible candidates for treatment outside bankruptcy in the future.

In fact, the government's decision to bail out Bear Stearns left many at Lehman, who expected similar treatment, to stand on the sidelines too long as bankruptcy neared. By the time these private actors realized Lehman would be left to go bankrupt, it was too late for them to implement many of the steps they could have taken to mitigate the resulting mayhem. (Despite getting off on the wrong foot, the Lehman bankruptcy managed to move quickly once begun, with Barclays able to buy up the failed firm's brokerage assets within the first week after the filing.)

Although the bankruptcy system, like all legal systems, can benefit from ongoing debate and evolution, it would be unwise to simply kill it off absent thoughtful discussion and good reason. Our leaders must exercise restraint when taking actions that will crowd out those who are adept at swooping into a failing or failed enterprise to turn things around or at least wind things up productively. When taking such steps they must also credibly delineate why ordinary bankruptcy rules are not being applied in a way that leaves ample room for our bankruptcy system to continue to operate with credibility in the future.

APPLICATIONS TO SOME CURRENT PROPOSALS

The central political problem faced by the Obama administration is that it doesn't want to overpay or to be the only one to blame if things go badly. Thus, it needs prominent partners from the private financial sector, who, however, have every reason not to participate. Why get into a partnership with someone who has mixed goals? The business of the private actors in our financial system is to make money by paying as low a price as possible for the assets in question and then reselling those assets at a higher price. The government (under administrations of either political stripe) is not out to make money, meaning its goals are hugely complicated and subject to change. In fact, the government has an incentive to overpay (as discussed above) because it wants to avoid leaving the banks under-capitalized and thus having to launch yet another program to purchase bank shares.

So how can the government gain political participation? It needs to get important groups in the private sector with large blocks of both political and economic power to decide to act in a coordinated fashion. And it needs to do so with enough self restraint that the fundamental rules of the game won't continue to change. We think this is all possible by focusing on mechanisms others have suggested for directly working through the core economic problems underlying the present crisis.

The most central economic problem of the current crisis is the large number of mortgages facing foreclosure that are held by ordinary citizens stretched too thin to adequately address their existing mortgage payments, especially in the face of declining home values. Estimates put the total number of such mortgages in the millions, covering a total amount of bad debt in the trillions of dollars. The prospect of carrying out so many foreclosures seems practically daunting and socially devastating. The people who own those homes face crushing challenges on the most human level. The financial entities that hold the mortgage notes and the many complex derivative instruments based on these notes appear to be carrying such huge losses on their books that they are unable to attract the new infusions of investment they need to enable them to contribute to the flows of financial credit the economy needs.

Not all these bad mortgages are of equal toxicity; many could be carried if a productive arrangement could be worked out. The uncertainty over sorting these out, however, is a significant factor driving down overall book values of banks.

Getting all these bad mortgages quickly and productively restructured or settled out involves a massive coordination problem, requiring participation by workout experts, mortgage holders, debtors, and owners of the derivative instruments. Clear rules that let all interested parties know that they must deal with one another and on what terms are the best way to get the needed collective action started and continued. Although the existing legal system, including contract law, property law, and bankruptcy law, provides an adequate framework, for reasons explored above, the chance that many of these rules will change freezes actors in place or encourages them to perhaps take steps that might help themselves but decrease the size of the overall pie. This means that the ongoing uncertainty associated with future commitments to act boldly is itself a factor contributing to the ongoing problem.

Furthermore, even immediately implementing some of the proposed reforms could be almost as risky. Consider for example the proposal to allow individual bankruptcy judges more leeway to cram down on the finance community on a case by case basis a lower amount than is due under existing loan contracts. First, putting these millions of cases through full-blown litigation is unlikely to increase the coordination speed. Second, for reasons explored above, such bold changes in bankruptcy law leave those who need to make new investments uncertain of the rules under which their deals will be judged. Third, it presumes that judges will be best able to figure out which mortgages can be productively carried by their debtors, even after restructuring, and which ones can still lead to serious failures.

In contrast, the ranks of professionals who are adept at turning things around or unwinding things can help, quickly and effectively, leveraging the private information held by the debtors, creditors, and others who are involved in each deal. If additional work is needed to bring all parties together quickly, then a proposal other than new power for bankruptcy judges might be in order. As suggested by Charlie Calomiris, the government could commit to bearing a percentage—perhaps 30 percent—of all write-downs reached by private agreement between the affected parties within a specified period of time, say six months. During the 1999 implementation in Mexico of the "Punto Final" (Final Point) program, private-sector actors came together quickly to take advantage of just such a joint subsidy approach. That joint subsidy approach would not only facilitate the needed coordination, but would also subsidize both the suffering home owners and the cash-strapped banks. At the same time, it would avoid both crowding out the professionals and scaring off those needed to invest in the reworked deals.

Conclusion

We recognize that many interesting ideas for short-term fixes to our present financial crisis have been offered. Not having endeavored to provide a thorough account of everything that has been written or tried on this important issue, we offer instead a single overarching point with a few practical implications that we fear have been largely overlooked during both the end of the Bush administration and the beginning of the Obama administration. Our hope is that pointing them out will help; once noticed they can be significantly mitigated at a low cost relative to the other approaches on offer. At bottom, we think it important for the government to very soon pick one set of institutions, and then stick to whatever it selects; for we fear that the costs of the uncertainties caused by ongoing change outweigh whatever benefits may come from tinkering further. Along the way, we pointed out one particular risk raised by present approaches, which is crowding out the many professionals in our private sector—consultants, financiers, lawyers, managers, and so on—who are expert at stepping into failed businesses and rework-ing or winding up affairs in a way that will redeploy assets toward more productive uses. Another risk is eliminating through the backdoor, and probably by accident, the ability for our well-estab-lished rules of bankruptcy to form the backdrop against which ongoing investments can be made. Although the bankruptcy system is far from perfect and discussions for improvement are encour-aged, tolling the death of bankruptcy at a time when new invest-ments are most needed is not the best approach.

2 Prudential Bank Regulation: What's Broke and How to Fix It

Charles W. Calomiris

Financial crises not only impose short-term economic costs but also create enormous regulatory risks. The financial crisis that is currently gripping the global economy is already producing voluminous proposals for regulatory reform from all quarters. Previous financial crises—most obviously the Great Depression—brought significant financial regulatory changes in their wake, most of which were subsequently discredited by economists and economic historians as counterproductive.

Since the 1980s, the United States has been removing many of those regulatory missteps by allowing banks to pay market interest rates on deposits, operate across state lines, and offer a wide range of financial services and products to their customers, thus diversifying banks' sources of income and improving their efficiency. It is worth remembering how long it took for unwise regulatory actions taken in the wake of the Depression to be reversed; indeed, some regulatory policies introduced during the Depression—most obviously, deposit insurance—will likely never be reversed. Ironically, financial economists and economic historians regard deposit insurance (and other safety-net policies) as the primary source of the unprecedented financial instability that has arisen worldwide over the past thirty years (Barth, Caprio, and Levine 2006; Demirguc-Kunt, Kane, and Laeven 2009; Calomiris 2008a).

Will the current regulatory backlash in response to the financial crisis once again set back financial efficiency, or will it lead to the refinement and improvement of our financial regulatory structure? As of this writing, a mixed outcome seems likely. Some changes in the content of banking regulation are likely to be constructive. In other areas—the reform of the regulatory use of rating agency opinions, and putting an end to the subsidizing of leverage in housing— the future is uncertain; counterproductive, knee-jerk reactions or preservation of the status quo, respectively, seem as likely as thoughtful reform. In some of the areas where reform would be desirable—most obviously, eliminating entry barriers in consumer banking—nothing is likely to occur. Finally, with respect to the implementation of supervision and regulation, major changes are afoot that will probably rearrange and consolidate financial oversight and extend the powers of the Federal Reserve Board into new areas. Reconsidering the allocation of regulatory power will likely bring a mix of unpredictable outcomes. Unfortunately, one desirable change—removing the Fed from its current role as a microsupervisor and regulator of banks—is unlikely to occur.

This chapter considers several important areas of response (or nonresponse) of banking regulation to the crisis. I begin with an overview of the causes of the crisis and the ways in which the crisis has highlighted the need for regulatory reform. I review the prospects for the reform of regulatory content. I also consider and evaluate the potential changes in the structure of regulation and supervision coming out of the crisis.

The Origins of the Crisis

Many commentators argue that the financial innovations associated with the securitization of subprime mortgages by banks and investment banks, and the repo finance of investment banks, permitted

subprime mortgage originators to sidestep commercial bank prudential regulation (of on-balance-sheet bank holdings of subprime
mortgages and related instruments) so that they could assume more
risk at lower cost by boosting leverage. There is no doubt that, had
more subprime loans been placed on the balance sheets of commercial banks, financial system leveraging would have been smaller. But
that would not have prevented the crisis. Government policies that
promoted risk taking in housing finance, and regulatory standards
for measuring risk when setting minimum capital requirements
(for banks, investment banks, and their securitizations), were far
more important in generating the hugely underestimated risks that
brought down the U.S. financial system.

As Calomiris (2009a) shows, on an ex ante basis, subprime
default risk was substantially underestimated during 2003–7. Reasonable, forward-looking estimates of risk were ignored, and senior
management structured compensation for asset managers to maximize incentives to undertake underestimated risks.

Those mistakes were not the result of random mass insanity;
rather, they reflect a policy environment that strongly encouraged
financial managers to underestimate risk in the subprime mortgage
market. Risk taking was driven by government policies. Four categories of government error were most important:

1. Lax monetary policy, especially from 2002 through 2005, promoted easy credit and kept interest rates low for a protracted
period. The history of postwar monetary policy has seen only two
episodes in which the real federal funds rate remained negative for
several consecutive years: the high-inflation episode of 1975–78
(which was reversed by the rate hikes of 1979–82) and the accom-
modative period of 2002–5. The Fed deviated sharply from the
"Taylor Rule" in setting interest rates during 2002–5; the federal
funds rates remained substantially and persistently below levels that
would have been consistent with that rule. Not only were short-
term real rates held at persistent historic lows, but unusually high
demand for longer term Treasuries related to global imbalances

flattened the Treasury yield curve during the 2002–5 period, resulting in extremely low interest rates across the yield curve. Accom-
modative monetary policy and a flat yield curve meant that credit
was excessively available to support expansion in the housing market at abnormally low interest rates, which encouraged the over-
pricing of houses and subprime mortgages.

2. Numerous housing policies promoted subprime risk taking
by financial institutions (Calomiris 2009a, 2009b). Those policies
included (a) political pressures from Congress on the government-
sponsored enterprises (GSEs), Fannie Mae and Freddie Mac, to
promote "affordable housing" by investing in high-risk subprime
mortgages, (b) lending subsidies for housing finance via the Federal
Home Loan Bank System to its member institutions, (c) Federal
Housing Administration (FHA) subsidization of high mortgage
leverage and risk, (d) government and GSE mortgage foreclosure
mitigation protocols that were developed in the late 1990s and early
2000s to reduce the costs to borrowers of failing to meet debt service requirements on mortgages, which further promoted risky
mortgages, and—almost unbelievably—(e) 2006 legislation that
encouraged ratings agencies to relax standards for subprime securitizations.

All these policies encouraged the underestimation of subprime
risk, but the behavior of members of Congress toward Fannie Mae
and Freddie Mac, which encouraged reckless lending by the GSEs in
the name of affordable housing, were arguably the most damaging
actions leading up to the crisis. For Fannie and Freddie to maintain
lucrative implicit (now explicit) government guarantees on their
debts, they had to commit growing resources to risky subprime
loans (Calomiris and Wallison 2008). Fannie and Freddie ended up
holding $1.6 trillion in exposures to those toxic mortgages, half the
total of non-FHA outstanding amounts of toxic mortgages (Pinto
2008).

3. Government regulations limiting the concentration of stock
ownership and the identity of who can buy controlling interests in

banks have made effective corporate governance within large banks virtually impossible. Lax corporate governance allowed bank management to pursue investments that were unprofitable for stockholders in the long run but were very profitable to management in the short run, given the short time horizons of managerial compensation systems. When stockholder discipline is absent, managers can set up the management of risk to benefit themselves at the expense of stockholders. An asset bubble (like the subprime bubble of 2003–7) offers an ideal opportunity; if senior managers establish compensation systems that reward subordinates based on total assets managed or total revenues collected, without regard to risk or future potential loss, then subordinates have the incentive to expand portfolios rapidly during the bubble without regard to risk. Senior managers then reward themselves for having overseen "successful" expansion with large short-term bonuses and cash out their stock options quickly so that a large portion of their money is invested elsewhere when the bubble bursts.

4. The prudential regulation of commercial banks and investment banks has proven to be ineffective. That failure reflects (a) fundamental problems in measuring bank risk resulting from regulation's ill-considered reliance on inaccurate rules of thumb, credit rating agencies' assessments, and internal bank models to measure risk, and (b) the too-big-to-fail problem (Stern and Feldman 2004), which makes it difficult to credibly enforce effective discipline on large, complex financial institutions (such as Citibank, Bear Stearns, AIG, and Lehman) even if regulators detect large losses or imprudently large risks.

The risk measurement problem has been the primary failure of banking regulation and a subject of constant academic criticism for more than two decades. Regulators use different means to assess risk, depending on the size of the bank. Under the simplest version of regulatory measurement of risk, subprime mortgages (like all mortgages) have a low asset risk weight (50 percent) relative to commercial loans, although they are riskier than those loans. More complex measurements of risk (applicable to larger U.S. banks) rely on the opinions of ratings agencies or the internal assessments of banks, neither of which is independent of bank management.

Rating agencies, after all, cater to buy-side market participants (i.e., banks, pensions, mutual funds, and insurance companies that maintained subprime-related asset exposures). When ratings are used for regulatory purposes, buy-side participants reward rating agencies for underestimating risk because that helps the buy-side clients reduce the costs associated with regulation. Many observers wrongly believe that the problem with rating agency inflation of securitized debts is that sellers (sponsors of securitizations) pay for the ratings; on the contrary, the problem is that the *buyers* of the debts want inflated ratings because of the regulatory benefits they receive from such ratings.

The too-big-to-fail problem involves the lack of credible regulatory discipline for large, complex banks. The prospect of their failing is considered so potentially disruptive that regulators have an incentive to avoid intervention. That ex post "forbearance" makes it hard to ensure compliance ex ante. The too-big-to-fail problem magnifies incentives to take excessive risks; banks that expect to be protected by deposit insurance, Fed lending, and Treasury-Fed bailouts and believe that they are beyond discipline will tend to take on excessive risk because taxpayers share the downside costs.

The too-big-to-fail problem was clearly visible in the behavior of large investment banks in 2008. After Bear Stearns was rescued in March, Lehman, Merrill Lynch, Morgan Stanley, and Goldman Sachs sat on their hands for six months awaiting further developments (i.e., either an improvement in the market environment or a handout from Uncle Sam). In particular, Lehman did little to raise capital or shore up its position. But when conditions deteriorated and the anticipated bailout failed to materialize for Lehman in September 2008 (showing that there were limits to Treasury-Fed generosity), the other major investment banks immediately were either acquired or transformed themselves into bank holding companies to increase their access to government support.

This review of government policy contributions to the financial crisis has not mentioned deregulation. During the 2008 election, many candidates (including President Obama) made vague claims that "deregulation" had caused the crisis. That claim makes no sense: involvement by banks and investment banks in subprime mortgages and mortgage securitization was in no way affected by banking deregulation. In fact, the deregulation of the past two decades (which consisted of the removal of branching restrictions and the expansion of permissible bank activities) facilitated adjustments to the subprime shock by making banks more diversified and by allowing troubled investment banks to become stabilized by becoming, or being acquired by, commercial banks (Calomiris 2009a). Since the election, President Obama and other erstwhile critics of deregulation have begun properly to focus on the various failures of regulation, rather than deregulation, as causes of the crisis.

Reforming the Substance of Regulation

The policy errors enumerated above were all subjects of substantial research before the financial crisis. It is not surprising, therefore, that credible solutions to those problems have been identified by financial economists who write about public policy. It is perhaps more surprising that the emerging academic consensus about reform is being embraced by Congress and the administration (at least so far). Even populist demagogues such as Barney Frank and Chris Dodd (who were egging on the pitchforks-and-torches crowd during the disgraceful AIG bonus hullaballoo) have shown some restraint in their regulatory reform advocacy.

Of course, the devil is in the details, and significant risks remain, including the possibility of counterproductive limits on compensation that could drive talent to less-regulated environments abroad, trading or reporting rules that would impose implicit taxes on the development of new derivatives products, barriers to competition masquerading as "stabilizing" regulation, and the empowerment of politicized regulators who would in turn politicize credit flows and other financial decisions.

No credible voice within the administration or Congress is pushing to repeal the 1999 Gramm-Leach-Bliley Act, which allowed banks unfettered entry into investment banking, although some (notably, Paul Volcker) have expressed the view that proprietary trading should be segregated from other aspects of banking. Barney Frank recently agreed with Chairman Bernanke during his testimony before Frank's committee, in particular with respect to the appropriate regulatory approach toward the hedge fund industry, which Bernanke argued should focus primarily on disclosure rather than regulatory control of hedge funds' risk or capital structure (the approach favored in much of continental Europe).

The emerging consensus reflects, inter alia, the Fed's ability to take the intellectual lead, thanks to its substantial staff resources and experience. Few in Washington have the wherewithal to dispute the Fed's knowledge and expertise on the technical matters of regulation. Having succeeded in elevating the discussion on regulatory reform, the Fed has given reformers (including myself) hope that this time government will not compound its errors too badly in its regulatory response to the financial crisis.

The following list summarizes sensible policy reforms (see Calomiris 2009b for details), many of which have been advocated by Secretary Geithner, Chairman Bernanke, and members of Congress and are reflected in the recent G20 declaration on regulatory reform (although the details the various parties will advocate remain uncertain):

1. Limit incentives for large, complex institutions to take advantage of too-big-to-fail protection by (a) employing regulatory surcharges on complexity (e.g., requiring higher capital or liquidity by

large, complex institutions) and (b) giving a financial regulator the authority to establish new procedures for intervening and resolving the problems of large, complex, distressed financial institutions (banks and nonbanks), rather than simply bailing them out. Secretary Geithner supports both elements. Some critics (e.g., Diebold and Skeel 2009) are legitimately concerned that discretionary resolution authority could lead to incompetent or politically motivated interventions. Other critics worry that defining an institution as "large and complex" might actually encourage bailouts. The answer to both problems is to require large, complex institutions to devise detailed and regularly updated plans to resolve their own problems. Those plans would specify how control would be transferred to a prepackaged bridge bank if the institution became severely undercapitalized and specify formulas for loss sharing among international subsidiaries of the bank (such loss-sharing arrangements would be preapproved by regulators in countries where subsidiaries are located). Credible, preapproved plans would discourage such banks from taking advantage of their large size and complexity to avoid discipline and would reduce the costs of too-big-to-fail protection. Such plans would also avoid the chaotic process of coordinating international loss sharing after the fact, in that the interests of different countries regulating different subsidiaries of troubled institutions often diverge (a major contributor to the chaos over the management of the crisis in Europe and the main remaining challenge to resolving the Lehman Bros. bankruptcy).

2. "Macro" prudential regulation is a relatively new idea that has been gaining support, including by Secretary Geithner, many in Congress, and the G20. A macro prudential regulator would vary capital and liquidity requirements over time in response to changes in macroeconomic and financial system circumstances. For example, during booms, minimum capital would be set higher, especially if a boom were occurring in which asset prices and credit were rising rapidly. Raising capital requirements on banks would discourage a protracted bubble from forming and create a larger

equity cushion for banks if a bubble should burst. Calomiris (2009b) reviews various ideas for setting dynamic capital requirements, arguing that it is possible to devise simple, desirable rules to implement such a policy.

3. Replace housing leverage subsidies with subsidies that carry less risk to low-income, first-time home buyers. Democrats in the House, Senate, and White House have not yet supported concrete measures that would reduce the vulnerability of housing finance going forward; many Democrats have, however, stopped claiming that Fannie and Freddie were mere victims of the crisis. The December 9, 2008, hearings in the House resulted in a bipartisan consensus that Fannie and Freddie had been major contributors to the crisis and that it is necessary to reform these institutions (which are currently in conservatorship). Given the huge political stakes, however, the prospects for reform are uncertain.

4. Use regulatory surcharges (capital or liquidity requirements) to encourage clearing of over-the-counter (OTC) transactions through clearinghouses, thus simplifying and rendering transparent counterparty risk in the OTC market. Secretary Geithner has advocated encouraging some migration of derivatives clearing to centralized clearinghouses (in fact, he championed the need to improve derivatives clearing when serving as president of the New York Fed). He seems to understand the need to distinguish between homogeneous derivatives products (like plain vanilla interest-rate swaps) that are good candidates for centralized clearing and other customized products that are not. Progress in bringing some derivatives products into clearinghouses has already been made.

5. Require timely disclosure of OTC positions to regulators and lagged public disclosure of net positions. This would help track systemwide risks by the macro prudential regulator and the market. The potential costs of too much disclosure or too rapid disclosure of positions are that such disclosures could reduce market liquidity under some circumstances (see Calomiris 2009b).

6. An important area that has not been much discussed by policy

makers is the need to reform the regulatory techniques for measuring risk. Secretary Geithner talks about the need for "capital, capital, capital," but more capital alone is not an effective solution; financial institutions can raise asset risk to offset higher capital requirements using various means, some of which are hard to detect. There is no substitute for effective risk measurement; yet ideas for reforming risk measurement have been missing in the congressional testimonies and speeches and G20 posturing, at least thus far. The most promising approach would be to use market prices to complement improved versions of existing measures of risk based on rating agency opinions and internal models. The key problem with the current approach is that it depends on bank reporting, supervisors' observations, and rating agencies' opinions. None of those three parties has a strong interest in accurate, timely measurement of risk. Furthermore, even if supervisors were extremely diligent in measuring risk, how could they successfully defend high risk estimates that were entirely the result of their own models and judgment? Part of the solution is to bring objective information from the market into the regulatory process and to bring outside (market) sources of discipline in debt markets to bear on bank risk taking. A large body of evidence favors that approach. The Fed and Treasury blocked that approach in 1999 (in response to lobbying pressure from the big banks), but Fed officials seem more amenable now.

7. Avoid grade inflation in rating agencies' opinions. Lots of bad ideas are surfacing about how to accomplish that goal, one of which is to require that the buy side pay for ratings rather than the sell side. As argued above, this would not improve the reliability of ratings. The regulated buy-side investors (banks, pensions, mutual funds, and insurance companies) pushed for ratings inflation of securitized debts to loosen restrictions on what they could buy; it is ludicrous to argue that giving the buy side more power would discourage ratings inflation. Another bad idea gaining ground in Europe is to have regulators micromanage the ratings process,

which would be destructive to the content of ratings. There are better alternatives, one of which would force ratings to be quantitative. Letter grades have no objective meaning that can be evaluated or penalized for inaccuracy. Numerical estimates of the probability of default (PD) and loss given default (LGD), in contrast, do have objective, measurable meanings. Rating agencies that provide ratings used by regulators (so-called NRSROs) should provide specific estimates of the PD and LGD for any rated instrument (they already calculate and report such statistics). Requiring NRSROs to express ratings using numbers could alter their incentives dramatically. If NRSROs were penalized for systematically underestimating risk over a significant period of time (say, with a six-month "sit out" from having their ratings used for regulatory purposes), they would have a strong self-interest in correctly estimating risk because the reduced demand for their services during the sit out would affect their fee income.

8. Change corporate governance rules to encourage better discipline of bank management. Rather than deal with the symptoms of poor governance in banks (e.g., compensation structure), it would be better to improve the ability of stockholders to discipline management. One such reform would be to eliminate ownership concentration limits on stockholders of bank holding companies, which would significantly improve their corporate governance.

Unfortunately, we are far from seeing legislation, much less sensible legislation, on most or all of the reforms listed, and there is substantial risk of mischief. But compared to the backlash we could be facing, the prospects for reform are reasonably good, with an encouraging absence of terrible ideas. Even the discussion on regulating compensation has so far focused on the need to align management incentives with long-term performance, rather than trying to limit the overall size of compensation.

Other desirable reforms, unrelated to the financial crisis, include, most importantly, permitting nonfinancial companies to enter consumer banking. Telecommunications and retail networks could provide cost-effective alternatives to bank branches and improve access for low- and middle-income consumers. That sort of deregulation was a long shot before the crisis; it is not a realistic near-term possibility.

Reallocating Regulatory and Supervisory Power

An area in which prospects for change are not favorable and on which economics is less helpful in guiding policy is the reallocation of regulatory and supervisory authority. The increased weight given to Fed opinions about reform may not be helpful here; the Fed's main goal in such debates has always been to preserve and expand its own authority, which has not generally been in the public interest (Calomiris 2006).

A lot is up for grabs in the reallocation of regulatory power, with one question being whether we should maintain the current system of multiple prudential bank regulators. The Office of the Comptroller of the Currency regulates national banks, the Fed regulates Fed-member, state-chartered banks, the FDIC regulates state-chartered, non-Fed member banks, the Office of Thrift Supervision regulates nationally chartered thrifts, and the Securities and Exchange Commission (SEC) regulates investment banks. Some critics fear that a "race to the bottom" could ensue as regulators compete to attract banks to their sphere of influence through lax standards. But the traditional view among banking historians has been that competition among regulators, who otherwise may be excessively prohibitive in their approach, fosters better regulation and supervision. Although no convincing evidence supports the race to the bottom argument, not much more evidence exists to support benefits from regulatory competition.

A second question is whether banking regulation should be compartmentalized (e.g., separating prudential regulation from consumer protection regulation) to improve enforcement. Aspects of prudential regulation may conflict with regulation designed to foster access (e.g., encouraging banks to tolerate greater risk when lending to low-income borrowers). Some advocates favor creating separate bodies for consumer and prudential matters so that each supervisory/regulatory body will have a clear, focused agenda. Others argue that combining consumer protection and prudential regulation in the same regulatory authority prevents regulators from issuing contradictory instructions.

Third, now that new regulatory actions relating to large, systemically important financial institutions are being proposed, where will those new authorities be housed? The Fed is perhaps the most likely choice. It possesses the resources and breadth of perspective to gauge risks and relevant trends in the economy better than any other macro prudential regulator. Furthermore, as the central bank and a lender to financial institutions, it already needs to maintain timely information about systemwide risk. The Fed is also a candidate for the new resolution authority (and is explicitly favored for that role by Barney Frank). Congress prefers to vest powers in the Fed because it exercises more control over the Fed than over other financial regulators. With respect to resolution powers and other new micro prudential authority, however, many strongly argue against expanding the Fed's role.

Indeed, policy makers should require the Fed to give up its role as a micro regulator, rather than expand that role through new resolution authority. Former secretary Paulson advocated reforms to remove the Fed from day-to-day regulatory and supervisory authority but gave it a new mandate to pursue macro prudential supervision and regulation.

Removing the Fed from micro regulation and supervision would have substantial advantages (Calomiris 2006). The United States is almost alone among developed economies in relying on its monetary authority as its primary day-to-day bank regulator and supervisor. The Fed not only sets and enforces prudential and consumer regulations but approves bank mergers and acquisitions and decides what constitutes permissible activities for banks. Why have other countries distanced their monetary authorities from such things? First, monetary authorities—especially when subject to political oversight by Congress, as the Fed is—may be less reliable regulatory enforcers. Second, combining regulatory powers with monetary authority politicizes monetary authorities, thus threatening independent monetary policy. Unfortunately, given the dominant role of the Fed in the current debates over the reallocation of power, there is little chance of distancing the Fed from the day-to-day responsibilities of supervision and regulation, despite the benefits.

CONCLUSION

Financial crises produce regulatory reactions, for better or worse, often for worse. The reforms in reaction to the current crisis have not yet been settled, and prospects for reform are mixed.

The most important desirable changes in regulation highlighted by the crisis would be (1) regulatory taxes and reforms of resolution processes that would discourage too-big-to-fail protection of large, complex banks, (2) macro prudential regulatory authority to gauge overall risk in the financial system and structure dynamic capital and liquidity requirements accordingly, (3) elimination of leverage subsidies in housing, (4) rules to encourage OTC clearing in clearinghouses, (5) disclosure standards for OTC market participants, (6) improvements in the measurement of regulatory risk that would include market-based measures, (7) changes in the use of rating agencies' opinions to discourage grade inflation, and (8) eliminating regulatory limits on the concentration of ownership in banks.

Items (1), (2), (4), and (5) seem likely to be implemented in some form, but the others are less certain. In areas unrelated to the crisis (most importantly, the relaxation of entry barriers in consumer finance) there is little hope of progress at the moment, and in many areas (e.g., new compensation rules) there is great potential for mischief from regulatory overreach; it is too early to be confident of measured reform.

With respect to reallocating regulatory and supervisory powers, important questions remain unresolved in theory and uncertain in prospect. One desirable reform—removing the Fed from day-to-day regulatory and supervisory decisions, especially in the most highly politicized areas of regulatory decision making—remains unlikely given the Fed's thirst for power, Congress's preference for vesting the Fed with power, and the Fed's growing influence in the current debates on regulatory reform. Indeed, if anything, the Fed's role as a micro prudential regulator is likely to grow, particularly through an expansion of its authority over the resolution of distressed financial firms.

References

Barth, James R., Gerard Caprio, Jr., and Ross Levine (2006). *Rethinking Bank Regulation till Angels Govern* (Cambridge: Cambridge University Press).

Calomiris, Charles W. (2006). "The Regulatory Record of the Greenspan Fed," *AEA Papers and Proceedings,* 96 (May): 170–73 (a longer version of the paper is at www.aei.org/publications/filter.all,pubID.28191/pub_detail.asp) .

Calomiris, Charles W. (2008a). "Banking Crises," *NBER Reporter* (National Bureau of Economic Research), no. 4: 10–14.

Calomiris, Charles W. (2008b). "Statement before the Committee on Oversight and Government Reform, United States House of Representatives," December 9.

Calomiris, Charles W. (2009a). "The Subprime Turmoil: What's Old, What's New, and What's Next," *Journal of Structured Finance,* forthcoming.

Calomiris, Charles W. (2009b). "Financial Innovation, Regulation, and Reform," *Cato Journal*, forthcoming.

Calomiris, Charles W., and Peter J. Wallison (2008). "The Last Trillion-Dollar Commitment: The Destruction of Fannie Mae and Freddie Mac," *Financial Services Outlook* (American Enterprise Institute), September.

Demirguc-Kunt, Asli, Edward Kane, and Luc Laeven, eds.(2009). *Deposit Insurance Around the World* (Cambridge, Mass.: MIT Press).

Deibold, Francis X., and David A. Skeel, Jr. (2009). "Geithner Is Overreaching on Regulatory Power," *Wall Street Journal*, March 27.

Pinto, Edward J. (2008). "Statement before the Committee on Oversight and Government Reform, United States House of Representatives," December 9.

Stern, Gary H., and Ron J. Feldman (2004). *Too Big To Fail: The Hazards of Bank Bailouts* (Washington, D.C.: Brookings Institution Press).

3 A Not-So-New Direction for Tax Policy

Kevin A. Hassett

During the past eight years, tax policy has been something of a political hot potato in the United States. Although President Bush accomplished only a few major domestic policy objectives in his two terms, the first and perhaps most notable was an across-the-board reduction in marginal tax rates, which should serve as a warning to those who draw too many conclusions from a president's early accomplishments.

Throughout the past eight years, opposition to the Bush tax cuts on high earners has practically been a membership requirement of the Democratic Party. Since 2004, every major Democratic presidential candidate, including our new president, has called for their repeal. To academics who study tax policy, the angry partisan tone of the debate has been highly ironic. As illustrated in Auerbach and Hassett (2005), among academics there is fairly broad agreement concerning the optimal design of tax policy.

Given the sweeping Democratic victory in November 2008, one might have expected the Bush tax reductions to have been quickly repealed. Circumstances, however, conspired to save the tax cuts, for a brief time at least. What is already the worst recession in postwar U.S. history has focused the attention of lawmakers on economic stimulus, with an ambitious plan becoming law.

The stimulus "distraction," however, has set the United States up for a truly momentous year in the history of tax policy. In 2010, virtually all of the Bush tax cuts will expire. Many of the expiring provisions are popular with Democrats and Republicans alike, and, hence, an important tax bill will inevitably emerge. Will that bill be a simple extension of the more popular preexisting policies or a reform that is guided by the academic consensus? The answer will depend on our new president's economic philosophy, which we can discover by drawing on the evidence from his first hundred days in office.

Any historical picture of the economic philosophy that animates a president must refer to changes he accomplished and changes he attempted but failed to accomplish. In the case of President Obama, we have already, in his first hundred days, a significant accomplishment to evaluate, as well as a fairly detailed view of his plans for the future. In the next section, I discuss the recent stimulus bill. In the subsequent section I turn to the president's budget, which details many of his plans for the future. I then discuss the tax panel that President Obama has assembled and the likely substantive effects of the charge that the panel has received. The final section is a conclusion.

THE STIMULUS BILL

President Obama signed the American Recovery and Reinvestment Act of 2009 into law on February 17, 2009. According to Recovery .gov (2009), the $787-billion package contained roughly $288 billion in tax relief and $499 billion in spending. This is the second stimulus package enacted since the beginning of the recession, which, according to the National Bureau of Economic Research (NBER) Business Cycle Dating Committee, began in December 2007 (NBER 2008). President Bush signed into law the first stimulus package, the Economic Stimulus Act of 2008, on February 13, 2008 (MSNBC 2008).

Before turning to the details, let us document the total tally for recent fiscal policy efforts (see figures 1 and 2, drawn from Hassett [2009]). Figure 1 is a comparison of the current path of government spending in the United States with that in previous recessions; figure 2 is a comparison of the likely reduction in tax revenues with previous countercyclical policies. Both figures suggest that government actions in this downturn are significantly greater than past efforts in the postwar period.

FIGURE 1

Federal Government Expenditure Increases in Response to a Recession (percentage point change in current expenditure as a percent of GDP after a recession trough)

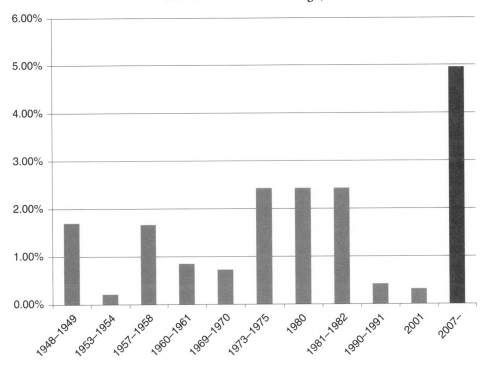

Sources: Congressional Budget Office; Bureau of Economic Analysis.

FIGURE 2
Major Countercyclical Tax Legislation Changes
during Postwar Recession Periods

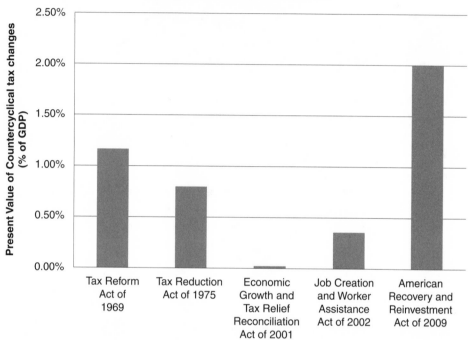

Source for first three bars: Christina D. Romer and David H. Romer, "A Narrative Analysis of Post-War Tax Changes" (University of California at Berkeley, November 2008; other sources: *Recovery.gov; Bureau of Economic Analysis.*)

Figure 3 is a comparison of the fiscal impact of actions taken in the United States with the impact of stimulus measures in Western Europe between 2008 and 2010. In each case, the total impact is scaled by gross domestic product (GDP). The figure indicates that European policy has been fairly restrained compared with that in the United States. Relative to GDP, the fiscal impact of the U.S. stimulus is nearly ten times larger than that of the French, almost double that of the Germans and significantly larger than that of even the most aggressive European country: Luxembourg.

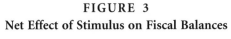

FIGURE 3
Net Effect of Stimulus on Fiscal Balances

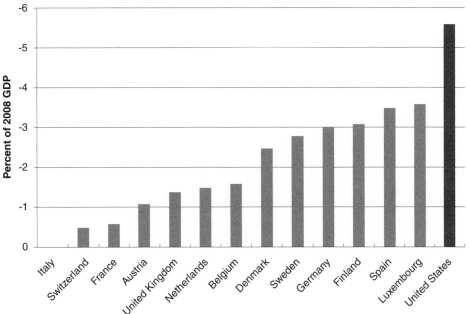

Source: "The OECD Economic Outlook Interim Report" OECD. March 2009. www.oecd
.org/dataoecd/3/62/42421337.pdf (accessed April 1, 2009).
Note: Figure shows the net effect of stimulus packages on fiscal balances for 2008–10 as
percentage of 2008 GDP.

Taken together, then, the figures imply that President Obama
has been more willing to pursue aggressive economic policy than
his predecessors and compatriots abroad. To the extent that this
tendency is a fixed effect, it implies that future policies may be
ambitious as well. In addition, the details of the stimulus bill provide
some evidence as to the likely shape of those future policies. I now
discuss each of these major details in turn. All cost estimates for the
American Recovery and Reinvestment Act of 2009 (ARRA) reflect
estimates released from the Joint Tax Committee (2009); all budget
estimates reflect the president's FY 2010 Budget, "A New Era of

Responsibility: Renewing America's Promise" (2009). I also draw heavily from analysis produced by the Brookings-Urban Tax Policy Center (Altshuler et al. 2009a; Altshuler et al. 2009b).

Expansion of credits

The Making Work Pay (MWP) credit, a central component of the tax measures included in the stimulus bill, is estimated to cost $116.2 billion over ten years. This refundable credit equals 6.2 percent of earnings and maximizes at $400 for individuals and $800 for couples. The credit phases out at a 2 percent rate over the income range of $75,000 to $95,000 for singles and $150,000 to $190,000 for married couples filing jointly. The legislation did not stipulate how the credit would be administered, but the conference committee report instructed the Internal Revenue Service (IRS) to distribute it through incremental withholding reductions rather than a lump sum refund. President Obama's 2010 budget proposed making the MWP credit permanent, which would cost an additional a $536.7 billion over ten years.

The stimulus bill also expanded several tax credits for low-income families. It increased the earned income tax credit (EITC) for working families with three or more children from 40 percent to 45 percent, the maximum credit amount from $5,028 to $5,657 for families with three or more children, and the income phase-out level for married couples. The total cost of the expansion is estimated at $4.7 billion; however, President Obama's 2010 budget proposes permanently extending this provision, which would cost $32.9 billion over ten years.

In addition, the income threshold for the refundable portion of the Child Tax Credit was lowered: under the new law, the credit phases in at earnings of $3,000, a substantial reduction from the previous level of $12,550 in 2009. The Joint Tax Committee (JTC) estimates the total cost of this extension to be $14.8 billion over ten years. The president's proposal to make the lower threshold permanent would cost an additional $70.5 billion over ten years.

The stimulus bill also expanded the home ownership credit to include additional incentives for first-time home buyers. It increased the maximum credit to $8,000 for married couples ($4,000 for married couples, filing separately) and allowed the credit to be delivered as a cash grant instead of an interest-free loan. The total cost of the credit is estimated by JTC to be $6.6 billion over ten years.

The American Opportunity Tax Credit, a new and partially refundable credit for postsecondary education, was also passed as part of the stimulus package. According to Altshuler et al., the credit is "equal to 100 percent of the first $2,000 plus 25 percent of the next $2,000 spent on tuition, fees, and course materials during each of the first four years of postsecondary education" (2009a). JTC estimates the cost of the stimulus provision to be $13.9 billion over ten years. The Obama budget proposes to make the credit permanent, costing an additional $74.9 billion over ten years.

Other individual provisions

This stimulus bill includes several temporary measures to aid the unemployed and encourage consumer spending, one of which exempts up to $2,400 of unemployment compensation from income taxation. This provision has received some criticism because workers would not realize the benefit until they file their 2009 tax returns in 2010. The total cost of this measure is estimated by JTC to be $4.7 billion over ten years.

Another attempt to encourage consumer spending in the legislation is a large deduction for automobile purchases. Vehicle purchasers would be allowed to deduct all state, local, and excise taxes paid on new vehicles (foreign or domestic) up to a purchase price of $49,500. The deduction would phase out over an income range of $125,000 to $135,000 for singles and $250,000 to $260,000 for married couples filing jointly. The provision is expected to cost $1.7 billion over ten years.

Although not considered "stimulative" by most tax policy analysts, ARRA extended the Alternative Minimum Tax (AMT) patch through 2009. The legislation indexes the 2008 thresholds for inflation, making the new threshold $46,700 for singles and $70,950 for married couples. The total cost of the AMT extension is estimated at $69.8 billion.

Business provisions

In the stimulus package, a number of provisions were targeted toward business activity. One such was the extension to 2009 of enhanced expenses for small business, which allows businesses to immediately expense the first $25,000 of investment in machinery and equipment; it will cost $41 million. In addition, the stimulus extends bonus depreciation, which allows businesses to write off half the value of their qualifying investment in the year of equipment purchase. This policy, which was relied on during the previous downturn as well, has an estimated cost of $5.1 billion.

Another provision would allow small businesses to carry net operating losses (NOLs) back five years to offset past income for any taxable year either beginning or ending in 2008. (Current law only allows for businesses to carry back NOLs two years.) The expansion of this tax provision will cost $900 million over ten years. Other smaller provisions include tax incentives to hire unemployed veterans and disconnected youth ($231 million over ten years), deferral of certain income from the discharge of indebtedness ($1.6 billion over ten years), tax-preferred "Recovery Zone Bonds" targeted to depressed areas ($5.4 billion over ten years), and an increase in the New Markets Tax Credit, a nonrefundable tax credit to investors who buy stock in companies investing in low-income areas ($815 million over ten years). The stimulus also generates $20 billion in new tax incentives for the development of alternative energy sources. (See table 1 for a summary of the costs of the main

TABLE 1
Tax Changes in President Obama's First Hundred Days
(numbers in billions)

Tax Measures	Cost over ten years(in billions)	Stimulus	Budget
Making work pay credit	$116	•	
	537		•
	653	•	•
Expansion of earned income tax credit	5	•	
	33		•
	38	•	•
Expansion of child tax credit	15	•	
	71		•
	85	•	•
American opportunity tax credit	14	•	
	75		•
	89	•	•
Home ownership tax credit	7	•	
Temporary suspension of taxation of unemployment benefits	5	•	
Automobile sales deduction	2	•	
AMT patch extension through 2009	70	•	
Enhanced expensing	0.04	•	
Bonus depreciation	5	•	
Expand NOL carryback	19	•	•
Other described business provisions	8	•	
Alternative energy development tax incentives	20	•	
Savers credit expansion and automatic enrollment in IRAs and 401(k)s	55		•
Eliminate advance EITC	− 1		•
Increase top two tax rates	− 339		•
Reinstate PEP and Pease	− 180		•
Increase tax rate on capital gains and dividends	− 118		•
Limit value of itemized deductions	− 318		•
Tax carried interest as ordinary income	− 24		•
Eliminate capital gains taxes on small businesses	7		
Reinstate Superfund taxes	− 17		•
Make R&E tax credit permanent	74		•
Implement international enforcement, reform deferral, and other tax reform policies	− 210		
Codify "Economic Substance Doctrine"	− 5		•
Eliminate LIFO accounting	− 61		•
Cap and trade	− 646		•
Total deficit change			
(in stimulus)	$287	•	
(in budget)	$ − 1066		•
Total for tax provisions	$ − 779	•	•

The table reflects tax code changes included in the stimulus and proposed in the president's FY 2010 budget. The net deficit decrease, however, is more than offset by proposed spending increases. The individual costs of the provisions do not sum to the total deficit changes. Total changes reflect Tax Policy Center estimates.

tax proposals enacted in ARRA and those proposed in the 2010 budget.)

The stimulus package revealed policy makers' willingness to pursue a wide range of policies designed to achieve social objectives, such as increasing access to home ownership and education. Policy makers also intentionally ensured that tax benefits went to the bottom of the income distribution, demonstrating their emphasis on the distributional aspects of tax changes. If one accepts the notion that low-income consumers are more likely to spend a higher share of their income, then one could back up these changes with economic stimulus arguments even if one were neutral toward redistribution. For evidence regarding economic stimulus, see Souleles (1999) and Lusardi (1996), who find that the marginal propensity to consume is higher for lower-income individuals.

BUDGET PROPOSALS

Presidents often signal their long-run policy objectives with their first budget proposal, and President Obama has done the same. To the extent that his economic policies are viewed as a radical departure from past practice, however, such departures must be attributed to nontax policies.

The president's budget proposed expanding the saver's credit by making it partially refundable for families with incomes below $65,000. Families with income below the threshold would be eligible for a 50 percent match on their first $1,000 of retirement savings, effectively paying half the cost of the first $1,000 saved in a retirement account. In addition, the president has proposed establishing automatic enrollment in IRAs and 401(k)s. The Office of Management and Budget (OMB) estimates the cost of these proposals to equal $55.2 billion over ten years. This proposal is perhaps motivated by recent evidence that such automatic enrollments can significantly increase saving behavior (Gale et al. 2005).

The budget proposal would also eliminate the Advance Earned Income Tax Credit, an option available to low-income workers with children who receive their EITC payments as a regular addition to their paychecks. This policy would provide an $882 million tax savings over ten years.

The president proposed a number of tax increases for high-income taxpayers. He plans to allow the Bush tax cuts to expire for the two top tax rates, allowing them to increase from 33 and 35 percent to 36 and 39.6 percent, respectively, in 2011. The tax rate increases would generate $338.7 billion in revenue over ten years. In addition, reinstating the personal exemption phase-out would reduce the value of each personal exemption from its full value by 2 percent for every $2,500 of income earned above a threshold. The limitation on itemized deductions ("Pease"), which reduces a taxpayer's itemized deductions by 3 percent of her or his income for all income over a threshold but not more than 80 percent, would also be reinstated. Both policies would affect couples with incomes levels of more than $250,000 and others with income more than $200,000. Reinstating the personal exemption phase-out and limitation on itemized deductions will generate an estimated $179.8 billion over ten years.

Other policies that would affect high-income taxpayers include increasing the tax rate of long-term capital gains and dividends from 15 to 20 percent and limiting the value of itemized deductions to 28 percent for taxpayers in the top two tax brackets, taxing carried interest as ordinary income. Those two policies would provide an increase in tax revenue of $118.1 billion and $317.5 billion, respectively. The budget also proposes to tax carried interest as ordinary income, a commonly used tax loophole for private equity and hedge fund managers that will raise an estimated $23.9 billion over ten years.

President Obama's 2010 budget proposes keeping the estate tax at its 2009 level instead of allowing it to disappear in 2010, as scheduled under current law. A major component of the wealth transfer tax reform that took place under the Economic Growth and Tax Relief Reconciliation Act of 2001 (EGTRRA) was the gradual phaseout of the estate tax by 2010 (Burman and Gale 2001). The president's budget proposes to keep the tax at the 2009 level: 45 percent for estates valued at more than $3.5 million ($7 million for couples). After the expiration of the Bush tax cuts in 2011, the estate tax is scheduled to resume at a rate as high as 60 percent on estates worth $1 million or more.

The budget also proposes a number of tax changes that would directly affect businesses. It proposes eliminating capital gains taxes on small businesses, costing $7.2 billion over ten years. It also proposes making the research and experimentation (R&E) tax credit permanent, which provides a 20 percent nonrefundable tax credit for all R&E above a certain threshold based on a firm's past R&E and annual gross receipts. The R&E tax credit has been included as a temporary provision in the tax code since 1981. The credit expansion will cost $74.5 billion over ten years. The budget proposes expanding the net operating loss carryback provisions, although how is as of yet unclear. It proposes to reinstate Superfund taxes on petroleum, chemical feedbacks, and corporate income to contribute to the Superfund trust fund, which is used to clean up contaminated sites. This would raise $17.2 billion over ten years.

The budget proposes closing offshore tax loopholes by codifying the "economic substance" doctrine (raising $4.9 billion over ten years), which states that a transaction must "have a meaningful economic purpose or investor risk" to be legitimate. Additional measures intended to stop tax haven abuse and strengthen international tax enforcement would raise $210 billion over ten years. Given the revenue estimate, this may signal the intention to significantly change laws that allow U.S. firms to defer U.S. tax on foreign earnings until they are repatriated. Furthermore, the budget proposes to eliminate last-in-first-out (LIFO) accounting, which creates a tax subsidy for corporations' inventory holdings; this will raise $61.1 billion over ten years.

The budget also proposes a "cap and trade" regime, in which corporations would buy permits allowing them to emit a predetermined level of carbon dioxide. In many respects, the regime is similar to a carbon tax and thus is worth a nod in this section. The total climate revenues raised would equal $645.7 billion over ten years, which implies that the actual program would recycle a good bit of the revenue through some unspecified tax reduction.

The U.S. tax code has evolved over time in to produce a narrower tax base and increased horizontal inequity (see Auerbach and Hassett [2002] for detailed evidence). Taken as a whole, the tax provisions contained in the 2010 Obama budget proposal accomplish much the same thing, signaling that the political forces that have led the tax code to wander so far from the economists' ideal are still present.

THE OBAMA TAX PANEL

It would be premature to judge from the first budget proposal that the Obama administration will continue to allow the tax code to stay in its wretched state. President Bush spoke frequently of tax reform and guided a process that produced, in 2005, a highly regarded study of the tax literature accompanied by specific tax proposals. One point of continuity is the attention given by the new administration to tax reform, recently highlighted by the establishment of President Obama's tax reform panel on March 25, 2009. President Obama has charged his economic recovery advisory board with recommending reforms to simplify a chaotic tax code and increase revenues.

It remains to be seen whether this effort will accomplish as little legislatively as the earlier one, but, at this juncture, the tax panel is worth reviewing in that its design may provide a glimpse of future policy proposals.

Although the panel's recommendations will not be released until the eve of the expiration of the Bush tax cuts (December 4, 2009), the panel's goals are to simplify the tax code, streamline credits, and generate additional revenues by closing the "tax gap," the difference between what taxpayers and companies owe and what they actually pay (Runningen and Donmoyer 2009). According to news coverage, White House budget director Peter Orszag, who has estimated the gap to be around $300 billion, explained that the panel aims to reduce "corporate welfare," which could mean that American companies would begin to be taxed on foreign income held abroad. The president has restricted the panel from recommending any tax increase for 2009 to 2010 or on families earning less than $250,000 per year (Runningen and Donmoyer 2009).

The panel's members come from both politics and academia. Paul Volker, current director of the national economic recovery board, will lead the panel, along with Austan Goolsbee, the appointed staff director of the task force. Other members include Martin Feldstein of Harvard University; Laura D'Andrea Tyson of the University of California at Berkeley; Roger Ferguson, a former vice chairman of the Federal Reserve; and William Donaldson, a former SEC chairman (Runningen and Donmoyer 2009).

George Bush's panel of tax experts evaluated the current tax code and recommended specific ways of making the "code simpler, fairer, and more conducive to economic growth" (Chamberlain 2005). The panel was headed by then Florida senator Connie Mac and Louisiana senator John Breaux. Other members included former congressman from Minnesota William Eldridge Frenzel, the Hoover Institution's Edward Lazear, former FTC chairman Timothy J. Muris, MIT's James Poterba, IRS commissioner Charles O. Rossotti, and LizAnn Sonders of Charles Schwab.

Given the wide consensus in the academic literature, it seems likely that the Obama panel will reach many of the same conclusions as the Bush panel. The Bush panel recommended two tax reform plans, the Simplified Income Tax Plan and the Growth and

Investment Tax Plan, each meeting the president's goals of simplification, fairness, and growth.

According to the commission's final report to Treasury secretary John Snow, both plans would accomplish the following:

- "[Simplify] of the entire tax system and [streamline] tax filing for both families and businesses.

- Lower tax rates on families and businesses, while retaining the progressive nature of our current tax system.

- [Extend] important tax benefits for home ownership and charitable giving to all taxpayers, not just the 35 percent who itemize; [extend] tax-free health insurance to all taxpayers, not just those who receive insurance from their employers.

- [Remove] impediments to saving and investment.

- [Eliminate] alternative minimum tax, which is projected to raise the taxes of more than 21 million taxpayers in 2006 and 52 million taxpayers by 2015."

Along with the elimination of the alternative minimum tax (AMT), the Simplified Income Tax Plan would reduce the number of statutory tax brackets from six to four and reduce taxes on the top bracket to 33 percent. Similarly, the Growth and Investment Tax Plan (GIT) proposed to eliminate the AMT and reduce the number of brackets to three and reduce the top tax bracket to 30 percent.

Both plans would replace the personal exemption, standard deduction, and child tax credit with the family credit, which would be available to all taxpayers. The family credit would include a $3,300 credit for married couples, a $2,800 credit for unmarried people with children, a $1,650 credit for singles, a $1,150 credit for dependent taxpayers, an additional $1,500 credit for each child, and a $500 credit for each additional dependent. The panel also proposed to replace the earned income tax credit with a "work credit," which would grant a maximum of $3,570 for working families with one child and $5,800 for families with two or more children.

The President's Advisory Panel also proposed substantial reforms that would make major credits and deductions available to all taxpayers, including the home mortgage credit that would equal 15 percent of mortgage interest paid. Both proposals would allow nonitemizers to deduct charitable contributions and all taxpayers to purchase health care with pretax money. The panel also proposed to simplify and consolidate existing education tax credits. An additional step toward simplification was consolidating fifteen different tax provisions for retirement, health, and education into three savings plans.

The Growth and Investment Tax plan, which closely resembled the income tax recommendations set forth in the Simplified Income Tax Plan but included additional reforms to the taxation of business and investment income, was a major step toward eliminating the inefficient taxation of savings and investment for households and businesses. The proposal planned to reduce the top rate for all businesses to 30 percent, matching the top rate on household income. The plan also allowed expensing for new business investments for large businesses and eliminated the deduction for interest paid and the taxation of interest received for large businesses. The plan would also tax dividends, interest, and capital gains received by individuals at a uniform rate of 15 percent.

Additional business proposals included a plan to simplify the requirements for small-business record keeping and a destination-based tax system featuring border adjustments (Chamberlain 2005).

President Obama's panel on tax reform

On December 4, 2009, President Obama's panel will present its final recommendations to the Treasury secretary; however, the president's campaign tax proposals along with his 2010 budget provide some indication of the reforms we can expect. Although these in many ways resemble the basic structure of the Bush proposals, the Obama budget proposals may tie the hands of the tax panel as they attempt to simplify the tax code.

Although credits, deductions, and their associated phase-outs generally add substantial complexity to the tax system, a significant consolidation of these items is unlikely. Indeed, the willy-nilly expansion of such things in the Obama budget dismays simplification advocates. The budget proposal's limitation on the value of itemized deduction at 28 percent, however, is a clever political tool that might be able to accomplish the base broadening favored by tax scholars. By collecting all the base-narrowing measures together, it may be that the political difficulty of reducing the state and local income tax deduction, mortgage interest deduction, and the like will be significantly reduced. If so, then such a measure may well be the centerpiece of a sensible income tax reform.

On the other hand, the Obama administration's 2010 budget proposes to make permanent several new credits aimed at benefiting low- and middle-income households. The new making work pay credit, included in the American Reinvestment and Recovery Act of 2009, is intended to offset payroll taxes by providing a credit of 6.2 percent of earnings up to $400 for individuals and $800 for couples.

But the cap on itemized deductions is similar to the 2005 President's Advisory Panel proposal to grant all taxpayers the same tax savings per deductible expenditure by "replacing itemized deductions with a 15 percent credit on most itemizable expenditures," thus separating the determination of ability to pay from the public value of the particular expenditure (Altshuler 2009b).

The last place to look for clues as to the likely direction of the panel is a recent tax reform proposal by panel codirector Austan Goolsbee to introduce a "simple return" that could significantly reduce compliance costs for taxpayers. The essential insight of

Goolsbee's plan is that the IRS already has all the necessary information to estimate the tax liability for most taxpayers; thus it would be a relatively simple step to require the IRS to take this information and send it in a pre-prepared tax form that the IRS to taxpayers (2006). By so doing, the IRS would allow each taxpayer to assess whether they are willing to accept that return or wish to correct inaccuracies by filling out their own. (The IRS's simple form would be correct for most taxpayers.)

Conclusion

The record of Barack Obama's first hundred days provides an incomplete picture of the new administration. On the one hand, the unprecedented stimulus package reveals an administration willing to take big economic chances; on the other hand, the flurry of traditional "targeted" policies that are anathema to tax scholars in the Obama budget suggests business as usual.

The president's tax reform panel, however, gives one reasonable cause for optimism because the charge of the panel seems broad enough to allow it to recommend sensible changes (similar to those recommended by President Bush's panel) and because the codirector of the panel is a key principal with a significant simplification plan already under his belt.

A final political consideration provides cause for optimism. The expiration of the Bush tax cuts will, of course, eliminate them, but most of the reductions, that is, those that affect individuals with incomes below $250,000, are popular with both parties. Accordingly, there will inevitably be an enormous tax bill to extend the popular provisions that will be a preexisting vehicle for the proposals of the president's commission. It is safe to say that the possibility of significant reform is higher than it has been in decades, provided that the new president is serious about the charge he has given his tax panel, not just nodding in the direction of reform by establishing a study group, as has so often been done in the past.

REFERENCES

Altshuler, Rosanne, Leonard Burman, Howard Gleckman, Dan Halperin, Ben Harris, Elaine Maag, Kim Rueben, Eric Toder, and Roberton Williams (2009a). "Tax Stimulus Report Card: Conference Bill," Brookings-Urban Tax Policy Center, February 13, 2009, www.taxpoli cycenter.org/UploadedPDF/411839_conference_reportc ard.pdf.

Altshuler, Rosanne, Leonard Burman, Howard Gleckman, Roberton Williams, and Dan Halperin (2009b). "Tax Proposals in the 2010 Budget," Brookings-Urban Tax Policy Center. February 2009, www.urban.org/ UploadedPDF/411849_2010_budget.pdf.

Auerbach Alan J., and Kevin A. Hassett (2002). "A New Measure of Horizontal Equity," *American Economic Review* (American Economic Association) 92, no.4: 1116–25.

Auerbach, Alan, and Kevin Hassett (2005). *Toward Fundamental Tax Reform* (Washington, D.C.: AEI Press).

Burman, Leonard, and William Gale (2001). "The Estate Tax Is Down but Not Out," *Urban Institute Tax Policies Issues and Options Policy Brief* (Brookings-Urban Tax Policy Center) no. 2: December, www.taxpoli cycenter.org/publications/url.cfm?ID = 310382.

Chamberlain, Andrew (2005). "Final Report of the Federal Advisory Panel on Federal Tax Reform" (Tax Foundation), Tax Policy Blog www.tax foundation.org/blog/show/1156.html.

Gale, William G., J. Mark Iwry, and Peter R. Orszag (2005). "The Automatic 401(k): A Simple Way to Strengthen Retirement Saving." *Tax Notes* 106, no. 10 (March 7): 1207–14. http://tpcprod.urban.org/ UploadedPDF/1000751_Tax_Break_3-7-05.pdf.

Goolsbee, Austan (2006). "The Simple Return: Reducing America's Tax Burden through Return-Free Filing." *The Hamilton Project* (Brookings Institution) www.brookings.edu/papers/2006/07useconomics_goolsbee .aspx.

Hassett, Kevin A (2009). "Why Fiscal Stimulus Is Unlikely to Work," *International Finance* 12, no. 1: 75–91.

Joint Tax Committee (2009)."Estimated Budget Effects of the Revenue Provisions Contained in the Conference Agreement for H.R. 1, The 'American Recovery and Reinvestment Tax Act of 2009'" JCX-19–09, February 12, 2009, www.house.gov/jct/x-19–09.pdf.

Lusardi, Annamaria (1996). "Permanent Income, Current Income, and Consumption: Evidence from Two Panel Data Sets." *Journal of Business & Economic Statistics* 14, no.1: 81–90.

MSNBC (2008). "Bush Signs stimulus Package into Law Rebates of $300 to $1,200 Go out Beginning in May," Associated Press, www.msnbc .msn.com/id/23143814/.

National Bureau of Economic Research (2008). "Determination of the December 2007 Peak in Economic Activity," (National Bureau of Economic Research Business Cycle Dating Committee), December, www .nber.org/cycles/dec2008.pdf.

Organization of Economic Co-Operation and Development (2009). "The OECD Economic Outlook Interim Report," March, www.oecd.org/ dataoecd/3/62/42421337.pdf.

Office of Management and Budget (2009). "A New Era of Responsibility, Renewing America's Promise" (White House), www.whitehouse.gov/ omb/budget/.

Recovery.gov (2009). "Relief for America's Working Families" (Recovery Accountability and Transparency Board), www.recovery.gov/.

Romer, Christina, and David Romer (2008). "A Narrative Analysis of Post-War Tax Changes" (University of California, Berkeley), November, http://elsa.berkeley.edu/~cromer/nadraft1108.pdf.

Runningen, Roger, and Ryan J. Donmoyer (2009). "Obama Asks Volcker to Lead Panel on Tax-Code Overhaul," Bloomberg.com, March 25, 2009, www.bloomberg.com/apps/news?pid = 20601087&sid = a_FIYIB VE5to&refer = home.

Souleles, Nicholas S. (1999). "The Response of Household Consumption to Income Tax Refunds." *American Economic Review* 89: 947–58.

Tax Policy Center (2009). "Tax Proposals in the 2010 Budget," www.tax policycenter.org/UploadedPDF/411849_2010_budget.pdf.

4   How *Not* to Invent a Patent Crisis

F. Scott Kieff and **Henry E. Smith**

A well-functioning patent system fosters innovation, creates jobs, and helps generate capital investment and overall economic growth. But a patent system can also be plagued by unnecessary and expensive court and administrative procedures and extreme uncertainty. Most patent reform proposals these days are designed to give officials and courts more power to weaken or eliminate "unworthy" patents, with so-called patent trolls as the bêtes noires du jour. No patent system is perfect, and our present system could be meaningfully improved. But in light of the rapid, and we would argue excessive, changes that have already occurred in the courts, what patent law needs is a tweaking of existing safety valves and processes—not opening the floodgates to more discretion and uncertainty.

Although a great deal of daylight may lie between the Bush and Obama administrations on a range of issues, when it comes to patent reform the bills brought before Congress during both administrations are remarkably similar, with the new bills introduced in early 2009, like those from 2007 and 2008, proposing significant changes to the patent statutes that have been in place since the 1952 Act.

During the past few years intense debates have brewed between those emphasizing the benefits of strong patents and those seeking to decrease baseless litigation and administrative process. Both groups raise important concerns and both have lobbied Congress and the White House in a curious set of political alignments. Those in the pro-patent camp are unions joining forces with Republicans and small businesses siding with big Pharma. Among the patent skeptics are the big players in High Tech joining with Democrats. Similarly, both the *New York Times* and The *Wall Street Journal* have advocated a major overhaul of patents (Timiraos 2007; Editorial 2007; Lee 2007; Sewell 2007; Fitzgerald 2007). The crowded reform bandwagon has a great deal of momentum.

The emerging consensus for flexibility targets three problems in current patent law. First is the concern with junk patents and the flood of patent applications at the Patent Office. Overworked and necessarily unaware of all the prior art that has preceded the patent applicants, examiners have let through a number of weak patents— leading to tales of patents for peanut butter sandwiches. Second, and relatedly, some industries are said to be subject to "anticommons" in which multiple rights overlap on the same subject (think gene fragments) also sometimes seen as "patent thickets" in which multiple patent rights need to be assembled to bring a product to market. We believe these two problems are overblown and can easily be handled within the framework of the 1952 Act, especially as supplemented by current case law. Third is the problem of "patent trolls," creatures who are notoriously hard to define or to spot in the wild. For some, a troll is any nonpracticing entity, a business that does not manufacture products covered by the patent. Such a definition threatens the specialization function of patents: Why should an inventor or even a company not be able to concentrate on research and development and leave manufacturing to others without running the risk of a being hit with a compulsory license? We recognize that a conceptually narrower problem does occur with patentees who induce reliance and then try to capture ex post the investments by the now-infringer. Sometimes these trolls are also called submarines, in that they surface and threaten to torpedo unsuspecting commercial traffic. But as we discuss in a moment, existing equitable safety valves are more than adequate to this task.

THE REFORM IMPULSE

Proposed reformers tend to fall into two groups. First are those who would alter the process to tighten the standard for granting patents, typically by giving some official or judge the discretion to decide what was within the skill of those in the prior art without being tethered (as heretofore) to factual inquiries into laboratory notebooks, printed publications, sample products, and the like. Such discretion-based proposals go by various names, including enhanced examination, opposition, reexamination, and second-window review. Second among reformers are those who would alter patent remedies, with injunctions being disfavored and more-tailored damages as the "solution."

Interestingly, recent U.S. Supreme Court decisions have already altered patent law greatly along the lines favored by the pro-flexibility reformers. The Supreme Court decision in the 2007 *KSR* case injected more discretion into the determination of obviousness, thereby making it easier to deny patents. The Court also has rejected, in the 2006 *eBay* case, the long-prevailing rule that a patentee with a patent adjudicated to be both valid and infringed should be able almost automatically to get an injunction; it now seems to require such a patentee to demonstrate its entitlement to an injunction on the more discretionary standard for obtaining injunctions from other areas of law. The Court has also, in the 2008 *Quanta* case, made it more difficult for patentees to license firms without at the same time licensing their customers.

All this amounts to a sea change in patent law, and all without a single revision to the patent statute. Although we certainly have bones to pick with some of these and other similar decisions, they do raise the question, Why don't we give them a chance to work (this was after all what advocates in those cases and of patent reform generally have told us those decisions were designed to do) before tinkering with the statute itself and its valuable, innovation-promoting architecture?

The best place to start considering the role—and drawbacks—of greater flexibility is in the central question of patent law: Does an invention satisfy the nonobviousness requirement for obtaining a patent? That is, in light of possibly far-flung and disparate pieces of prior art, is the invention something that a person having ordinary skill in the art would have already been just about to do—or not?

The 1952 Act makes prior art largely a question of fact, based on evidence such as documents and factual testimony, as compared with opinion testimony. Some see the recent *KSR* decision as standing for the proposition that government decision makers such as judges now have increased discretion to pronounce what the prior art teaches and would like to extend such discretion to patent examiners. Others think the case was narrowly decided on its facts and that the relevant inquiry remains an objective determination of precisely what was taught by the particular combination of relevant pieces of prior art (Epstein and Kieff 2007; Haber, Kieff, and Paredes 2007).

Importantly, proposed statutory changes would implement the same flexible approach urged by one side of the *KSR* debate. We think that flexibility can be carried too far and that the flexibility approach on offer relies on two false premises about how the system actually works.

The first false premise is that beefing up the patent examiner's resources would help her find the key prior art. Of course, our examining corps should have good access to Internet databases and ample time and training to peruse them. But no realistically available amount of time and training will help an examiner at his desk obtain the laboratory notebook of an individual researcher at some company or university or an obscure student thesis on the bookshelf of a foreign library, which is where the key prior art is often found.

The second false premise is that discretionary decision making, whether in court or the Patent Office, can be immune from political and other pressure. Asking a decision maker to use her legal or technical expertise as the primary basis for deciding what she thinks the state of the art was at a particular time in history gives her greater discretion than asking an ordinary jury whether a particular document or sample product existed at a particular time and what that document actually contains. By increasing the discretion of government bureaucrats, flexibility increases uncertainty and gives a built-in advantage to large companies with hefty lobbying and litigation budgets.

LESSONS FROM HISTORY

The historical consensus about patents turns out to be the exact opposite of today's. Concepts such as across-the-board flexibility, balance, discretion, and subjectivity are not new to our patent system; we've tried them before, in ways strikingly similar to those proposed today. They were the hallmarks of the patent systems of the 1940s and of the 1970s, and, although the product of well-intentioned efforts, the results in each setting were consistent and bad.

Like other proposals to deal with our current crises, dialing down the patent system gained steam in the New Deal. Created in 1938, President Roosevelt's Temporary National Economic Commission specifically targeted patents under the misguided belief that they led to the "concentration of economic power" (Public Resolution). By a decade later, the entire patent system had become practically decimated by the courts.

Determinations about a patent's validity in those days typically boiled down to a flexible but tautological standard: to be patentable, an invention had to constitute what a judge considered to be an "invention." Some courts, including the Supreme Court in its

1950 *A&P* case, treated this as a "synergism" test under which patents would be valid only when the claimed invention combined existing elements to achieve a mystically synergistic effect. The test became so vague and difficult to satisfy that Justice Jackson remarked in the 1949 *Jurgensen* case that "the only patent that is valid is one which this court has not been able to get its hands on."

At the same time, a patentee's options for licensing or bringing infringement suits were severely curtailed throughout the 1930s and 1940s as courts virtually eliminated the patent law doctrines that hold a defendant accountable for causing infringement by third parties. By the late 1940s, the Supreme Court was seeing patent misuse and antitrust concerns everywhere.

In response, Congress passed the 1952 Patent Act, which aimed to reverse the Supreme Court's expansive approach to patent misuse and set forth an objective test for patentability called "nonobviousness." Avoiding the usual process of extensive interest-group lobbying, leading to "balance" in the sense of brute compromise, the 1952 Act represented the consensus views of legal technicians interested in developing a system that was balanced in the different sense of logical coherence. In 1948 the New York Patent Law Association asked its past president, Giles Rich, to draft a bill that would provide a more predictable framework for patent law. Rich collaborated with a Patent Office representative named Pat Federico to draft a bill, coordinate national discussion of the issues, and explain them to Congress. The result was the 1952 Act, which substantially remains the patent law today.

The 1952 Act was applauded for its predictability by the leading jurists and commentators of the time, such as Learned Hand and Jerome Frank of the New York-based U.S. Court of Appeals for the Second Circuit. Judge Hand had repeatedly called for courts to determine patent validity objectively. As he explained in the 1946 *Safety Car Heating & Lighting* case when criticizing the absurdity of the synergism test: "substantially all inventions are the combination of old elements; what counts is the selection, out of all their possible

permutations, of that new combination which will be serviceable."
Writing later, Giles Rich went further, explaining that a synergism
test makes no sense because "[t]he laws of physics and chemistry
in accordance with which all inventions perform do not permit of
the judicially imagined magic according to which $2 + 2 = 5$" (Rich
1972). Judge Frank put the net impact of the more objective
approach very simply in the 1942 *Picard* case when he explained
how patents produced by such a system can be the vital slingshots
smaller innovative "Davids" use to compete against large established "Goliaths."

Although the progress made by the 1952 Patent Act had been
seriously eroded by the end of the 1970s, leaders from both sides of
the political aisle soon acted to reinvigorate patents. A key figure
from the patent system of the 1970s, Pauline Newman, then head
of chemical giant FMC Corporation's patent operation and now a
judge on the Federal Circuit, has been reminding policy makers and
commentators for years that the push to re-strengthen the patent
system that culminated in the 1982 act signed by President Reagan
was the direct result of a serious effort launched by President Carter
(Newman 2005). The 1982 act created the court on which judge
Newman now sits: the Federal Circuit, which hears the appeals
from most patent cases across the country. By 1978, when the economy had reached serious disarray, President Carter, through his
Commerce Department, empanelled a group of experts to conduct
a "Domestic Policy Review" to study domestic innovation. Its key
findings focused on the destructive impact on commercializing
innovation and economic growth caused by unpredictability in the
patent system; its chief recommendations included strengthening
the patent system through the increased predictability that could be
implemented by a new court (Industry Subcommittee 1979).

We have now come full circle—again. After a consensus era of
strong patent protection, the Supreme Court's recent decisions,
especially the current reform proposals, are back to the future. Why

not learn from the twentieth-century history of patents, instead of repeating it?

IMPROVING THE PATENT SYSTEM

Much of the impulse for root and branch change comes from an incomplete view of what the patent system does and how it does it. Proponents of flexibility measure the system's success by how well it achieves the "correct" reward for inventions. The ideal benchmark would be an all-knowing planner who would hand out checks in the exact minimum amount to induce the invention in question—and in any event no greater than the invention's social value. What all this overlooks is that the system does more than provide a reward for invention; it also provides an overall architecture for innovation.

Getting an invention made and bringing it to market require coordination among its many complementary users, including developers, managers, laborers, other technologists, financiers, manufacturers, marketers, and distributors. Patents help achieve this socially constructive coordination by allowing those various actors to interconnect with each other like modules of a larger system. The underlying mechanism depends in at least three fundamental ways on the expectation that patents will be enforced with strong property protection. First, the credible threat of exclusion associated with a published patent acts like a beacon in the dark, drawing to itself all those interested in the patented subject matter. The beacon effect motivates those diverse actors to interact with one another and with the patentee, starting conversations among the relevant parties. Second, the widespread expectation that the patent will be enforced motivates each of these parties to reach agreements with one another over the use and deployment of the technology. That bargaining effect falls apart if the parties are unsure that the patent will be enforced; if the patent is seen as not being enforced, there is significantly less need to reach agreement ex ante. Thus the fear of weak enforcement creates a disincentive for the necessary parties to work together at the outset. Finally, patent protection allows patentees to appropriate the returns to (rival) inputs to developing and commercializing innovation—labor, lab space, and so forth—without the law having to trace the relative contributions of these multifarious inputs. Instead patents form a platform on which coordination and development can take place (Kieff, 2007; Smith 2007).

But when it comes to evaluating the system, today's proponents of flexibility tend to treat it as a bundle of features or levers that can be tweaked on an industry-by-industry or even a case-by-case basis. How high should the bar for patentability be? What should the size of the reward be for a contribution? Would an injunction lead to too much bargaining power? The list goes on and on.

As we have seen, those designing and implementing our present patent system realized that many of the benefits of patents could be achieved holistically. The benefits in terms of stability and coordination from the system are not results achieved by this or that part of the system, which could be better tailored by greater levels of official discretion, in the interest of wringing out all the errors from the system.

The current consensus for flexibility problematically—and ironically—deals in absolutes. If the system does not provide good notice all the time, it is "not doing its job" and thus any change is presumptively an improvement. Theoretical problems with multiple patents impeding commercialization were declared an impending disaster before any empirical investigation. Modest problems along these lines exist, but their very modesty suggests that altering the mix of certainty and flexibility is better than declaring the system a failure and opening the flood gates of discretion (Murray & Stern 2007; Walsh et al. 2004).

This is not to say that the system cannot be evaluated empirically or that it cannot be improved. But it does suggest caution and creativity in evaluating the case against the system and for radical reform. Although we think the flexibility-based solutions offered by patent critics are imprudent, some of the underlying concerns they raise are important to address. Here are our proposals.

Remove the presumption of patent validity. The patents that drive most calls for reform are indeed pernicious because they allow patentees to threaten expensive but meritless litigation against competitors, although the extent to which the U.S. patent system is afflicted with a disproportionate number of "bad" patents is a topic of serious debate (Katznelson 2007). Under the present system, an issued patent is presumed valid, which requires a challenger to prove invalidity by a higher standard of proof ("clear and convincing evidence") than usually prevails in civil cases ("preponderance of the evidence").

The costs under the present system of knocking out even an obvious patent can be large. The infamous litigation over Amazon's "one-click-shopping-patent" probably required Barnes and Noble to spend more than two million dollars in litigation costs alone to defeat the preliminary injunction that had wreaked havoc during the 1999 Christmas season rush. The threat of such expensive litigation over even a questionable patent is precisely what is said to terrorize potential defendants, large and small, about the present patent system. But this *in terrorem* problem can be greatly mitigated through more targeted measures than injecting large dollops of discretion.

Dialing down the present presumption of validity to something like the ordinary standard for civil cases would decrease the bad, *in terrorem*, effect. When litigation is needed, the carefully crafted Federal Rules of Civil Procedure govern the procedures for joinder, compulsory counterclaims, and against relitigating issues and claims decided in previous litigation, which are collectively designed to avoid abusive and repetitive process. The Federal

Rules also provide streamlined procedures such as summary judgment, which avoids long trials where there is no genuine issue of material fact.

In the end, a decrease in the presumption of validity would be particularly good for the "Davids," because it directly protects them from the *in terrorem* effect of junk patents and the threat of expensive but baseless litigation to defend against patents whose "validity" rests entirely on the present presumption. It also indirectly helps them raise the funds needed to litigate against a baseless opponent, regardless of whether they are asserting patent infringement or invalidity.

Some may argue that increasing the reliance on opinions of counsel will make it harder for lawyers to give advice, which is where the old tension underlying attorney-client privilege comes into play. On the one hand, decision makers often need to verify whether a party acted with good advice of counsel. On the other hand, it will be hard for a lawyer and client to openly discuss the strengths and weaknesses of various approaches if they know that all their communications are likely to be subject to open review later in court. But this is a false dichotomy. One lesson our society has learned from corporate scandals such as Enron is that it can be important to decouple auditing from advising. An opinion of counsel about a patent can be an important auditing tool that should be kept separate from the important advising resources a client needs in the competitive market and in litigation. This distinction should motivate the Federal Circuit as it works to clarify the evolving case law relating to attorney-client privilege for patent opinions of counsel after the 2004 *Knorr* case. Also, to prevent opinions of counsel from becoming a box to check and a whitewash for misconduct, courts have shown little hesitance to sniff out bogus opinions of counsel or to specifically call out their authoring attorneys and law firms, as was done by both the trial and the appellate courts in their respective 1997 and 1998 decisions in *Johns Hopkins v. CellPro.*

Institute symmetric fee shifting. Imagine a patent system in which both patentees and potential infringers had good access to fee shifting when the other side's case was baseless. Under today's rules, the patentee wants to educate the alleged infringer about the strength of the infringement case early in the process because this increases the patentee's chance of getting enhanced damages, such as attorney fees. For the same reason, the alleged infringer has a strong incentive to avoid notice by avoiding communication.

Symmetric fee shifting would allow alleged infringers to collect attorney fees from a patentee who brings an infringement case after having been warned, for example, about a particular item of invalidating prior art. This practice of fee shifting when a patentee makes baseless arguments in defense of the patent's validity would match the present rules in Sections 284 and 285 of the statute that allow patentees to get fees and (potentially) treble damages from infringers who should have known about their own infringement and have thus mounted baseless arguments in their defense. Such symmetry in fee shifting would encourage parties to exchange information and resolve disputes before undertaking expensive litigation (Kieff 2003; 2009). Under our rule, the alleged infringer would similarly want to educate the patentee about any validity-destroying prior art. Symmetry in fee shifting helps align both parties' incentives to communicate with each other.

Such a system would mean that the existing markets for audit-type opinions of counsel would grow. Under today's rules, the alleged infringer often wants to get an opinion of counsel early in the process so as to bolster later arguments that it had a good-faith basis for believing it had not infringed valid patent rights, thereby decreasing the chances of paying enhanced damages or attorney fees if it loses the case. Using our rule, the patentee would also want to get an opinion of counsel early in the process to establish its good-faith basis for its position, so as to avoid having to pay the alleged infringer's attorney fees.

Under our proposed practice, it will be easier for third parties to essentially spread the costs across multiple customers by opening businesses that provide rating services like those seen in today's capital markets that evaluate a particular company's stock or bond offerings. The ability to get attorney fees in baseless cases also opens up the market for contingent and other flexible fee arrangements for those who are too liquidity constrained to fight on their own.

Equity in remedies. Injunctions have come under a lot of fire, and recent flexibility-based reform proposals have centered on substituting tailored damages for injunctions in patent cases. Most of the time injunctions provide the certainty needed to avoid disputes and, when disputes do arise, encourage the parties to resolve them early. With injunctions, infringers have a hard time gaming the system or using the possibility of undercompensatory damages to do an end run around negotiations. Infringement is the violation of a property right; an injunction forces the infringer to stop and enforces the delegation of valuation questions to patentees and their contractual partners, with a view toward markets for inputs and products, rather than officials, courts, and experts for hire (Kieff 2001; Smith 2009).

But as illustrated by the furor over trolls, injunctions have their limits. When an infringer in good faith makes large, irreversible investments that include reliance on a patent that would have been easy to design around ex ante but hard to do so ex post, the infringer does have a claim on our sympathies (Denicolò et al. 2008). But contrary to what critics sometimes claim, this problem does not distinguish patent law from tangible property, which faces the same problem. In building encroachments, the good-faith encroacher—for example one building close to the lot line in reliance on a faulty survey—can argue against an injunction and pay only damages. But this emphatically does not apply to bad-faith encroachers: those who know they are committing a wrong. Many in the patent reform camp claim that patent law is not like property because it fails to give notice of claims: patent law cannot capture inventions in language, and patents are too hard to find (Bessen and Meurer 2008). We think the reforms we have discussed would, by providing individualized notice, help ensure that others infringe (if at all) in bad faith. Another possible rule is that for those cases of infringement that are based on the doctrine of equivalents, which extends the literal claims to cover a penumbra of hard-to-foresee additional invention space, in the remedy should be presumed (strongly) to include only damages, not an injunction (Smith 2007).

But introducing *more* discretion into determinations of patent validity is exactly the wrong way to go. For the inevitable uncertainty and difficulty in giving notice that remain (in real property law too, more than patent skeptics acknowledge), traditional equitable principles are more than up to the job.

The 2006 Supreme Court *eBay* decision held that the standard for an injunction is based on a four-factor test applied in other settings, without much further guidance. Taking their cue from the concurrences in the case, some see this as an invitation to inject more discretion to withhold injunctions in the broadly defined public interest. Others see the case as largely confirming a strong tendency toward injunctions, once validity and infringement have been decided in court.

We think that the best way to implement *eBay* is to take this equitable approach seriously and apply it in the traditional (and sensible) fashion. Crucially, the equitable approach is a safety valve for those situations in which someone who is otherwise a good candidate for getting an injunction—such as a patentee whose patent has been infringed—should not get one because of some glaring injustice. The equitable approach is flexible but not boundlessly so, in contrast to currently proposed reforms that elevate discretion to new heights. Moreover this safety valve is probably all we would need.

First, the order of the factors in the test—irreparable harm, inadequacy of damages, balance of hardships, and public interest—is no accident. In the old days when courts of equity were separate from courts of law, the inadequacy of the legal remedy (here damages) because of irreparable harm was jurisdictional. There is a functional reason for this as well: equity is a safety valve, not an ocean of free-floating discretion. It is designed to be effective only within a limited domain where it's most needed and will not upset general expectations.

Turning to the balance of hardships and public interest, these two factors sound a lot broader than the safety valves they are meant to be. The balancing called for in the traditional equitable test is not a full-blown cost-benefit analysis or an even a weighing of hardship of both sides. Instead, traditional equitable analysis asked whether someone otherwise entitled to an injunction should not get one, in the judge's discretion, in light of a *grossly disproportionate hardship* on the defendant (Epstein 1997; Schwartz 1964; American Jurisprudence 2d Injunctions 2005). The point here is not to get the exact correct reward but to avoid egregious errors in an otherwise robust system of injunctive relief.

Likewise, the public interest standard in equity is not an invitation to maximize official discretion. Rather, it is another safety valve to prevent major harm to third parties. Judges are simply not able to measure the public interest in some more specific fashion, such as a cost-benefit analysis or the judges' values or who knows what.

Finally, the equitable approach embraces more than this four-factor test. Injunctions can be tailored to the harm and delayed to give an innocent infringer time to redesign (Lemley and Shapiro 2007). And a delay in suing or lurking in wait while good-faith reliance occurs can sometimes be grounds for denying injunctions.

CONCLUSION

The approach we propose will decrease slightly the average value of all patents because patentees will now have to fight harder on the issue of validity when they assert their patents in court. But this is not necessarily bad. The costs of arguing to the Patent Office to get patent rights in the first instance will be less than in a system under which the examiners have largely unfettered discretion to reject applications.

Most important, the approach we propose directly addresses the fears of those held hostage under the current system by the threat of litigation costs surrounding patents that are merely presumed to be valid. Under a decreased presumption of validity, such a terrorizing effect largely evaporates. With fee shifting, meritless suits against infringers will be discouraged, and the full traditional but limited use of equitable discretion will provide all the safety valves we need for good-faith infringers and those facing true patent trolls. These approaches should be given time to work. The prudent course for the country is to embrace a strong patent system based on predictability and facts, which will benefit all players, large and small, in their contributions to American innovation and economic growth.

REFERENCES

American Jurisprudence 2d Injunctions, v. 42, § 35 (2005).

Bessen, James, and Michael J. Meurer. *Patent Failure: How Judges, Bureaucrats, and Lawyers Put Innovators at Risk,* pp. 29–72 (Princeton University Press, Princeton, NJ, 2008).

Denicolò, Vincenzi, et al. "Revisiting Injunctive Relief: Interpreting *eBay* in High-Tech Industries with Non-Practicing Patent Holders," *Journal of Competition Law and Economics,* v. 4, p. 571 (2008).

Editorial. "Patent Bending," *Wall Street Journal,* June 9, 2007, A8.

Epstein, Richard A. "A Clear View of *The Cathedral*: The Dominance of Property Rules," *Yale Law Journal,* v. 106, pp. 2091, 2102 (1997).

Epstein, Richard A., and F. Scott Kieff. "Flexible Patent Law . . . and Its Achilles Heel," *Wall Street Journal,* May 11, 2007, A19.

Fitzgerald, Michael. "A Patent Is Worth Having, Right? Well, Maybe Not," *New York Times,* July 15, 2007.

Haber, Stephen, Scott Kieff, and Troy Paredes. "Patent Reform Legislation: No Final Cut for Examiners," *National Law Journal,* May 14, 2007.

Industry Subcommittee for Patent & Information Policy, Advisory Committee on Industrial Innovation. *Report on Patent Policy,* p. 155 (1979).

Katznelson, Ron D. "Bad Science in Search of 'Bad' Patents," *Federal Circuit Bar Journal,* v. 17, p. 1 (2007).

Kieff, F. Scott. "Property Rights and Property Rules for Commercializing Inventions," *Minnesota Law Review,* v. 85, p. 697 (2001).

Kieff, F. Scott. "The Case for Registering Patents and the Law and Economics of Present Patent-Obtaining Rules," *Boston College Law Review,* v. 45, p. 55 (2003).

Kieff, F. Scott. "On Coordinating Transactions in Information: A Response to Smith's Delineating Entitlements in Information," *Yale Law Journal Pocket Part,* v.117, p. 101 (2007).

Kieff, F. Scott. "The Case for Preferring Patent Validity Litigation over Second Window Review and Gold Plated Patents: When One Size Doesn't Fit All, How Could Two Do The Trick?," *University of Pennsylvania Law Review,* v. 157 (2009).

Lee, Timothy B. "A Patent Lie," *New York Times,* June 9, 2007.

Lemley, Mark A., and Carl Shapiro. "Patent Holdup and Royalty Stacking," *Texas Law Review,* v. 85, pp. 1991, 2037–38 (2007).

Murray, Fiona, and Scott Stern. "Do Formal Intellectual Property Rights Hinder the Free Flow of Scientific Knowledge? An Empirical Test of the Anti-Commons Hypothesis," *Journal of Economic Behavior and Organization,* v. 63, p. 648 (2007).

Newman, Pauline. "The Federal Circuit in Perspective," *American University Law Review,* v. 54, pp. 821, 822–23 (2005).

Public Resolution No. 113, 75th Cong. (1938).

Rich, Giles S. "Laying the Ghost of the 'Invention' Requirement," *American Patent Law Association Quarterly Journal,* v. 1, pp. 26, 44 (1972).

Schwartz, Herbert F. "Injunctive Relief in Patent Infringement Suits," *University of Pennsylvania Law Review,* v. 122, pp. 1025, 1045–46 (1964).

Sewell, Bruce. "Patent Nonsense," *Wall Street Journal,* July 12, 2007, A15.

Smith, Henry E. "Intellectual Property as Property: Delineating Entitlements in Information," *Yale Law Journal,* v. 116, p. 1742 (2007).

Smith, Henry E. "Institutions and Indirectness in Intellectual Property," *University of. Pennsylvania Law Review,* v. 157 (2009).

Timiraos, Nick. "Businesses Battle over Patent Laws," *Wall Street. Journal,* June 9, 2007, A7.

Walsh, John P., et al. "Effects of Research Tool Patents and Licensing on Biomedical Innovation," in *Patents in the Knowledge-Based Economy,* edited by Wesley M. Cohen and Stephen A. Merrill. (National Academies Press, Washington, DC, 2004).

5 At What Price, Green?

Terry L. Anderson and Gary D. Libecap

Although the Obama administration has been fixated on bailouts and stimulus, it has not lost sight of the fact that its campaign promises included a dramatic change in environmental policies. Reacting especially to the Bush administration's apparent unwillingness to grapple with global warming and energy issues, President Obama has taken the same bold steps on these issues that he has on other headline issues.

Rather than trying to cover the entire range of policies, we focus our analysis on the major issues of climate change and green jobs, the two areas where the administration is putting its environmental emphasis. Our major points are (1) that the administration has not been candid with the American public about the costs of these initiatives or about the likelihood of their ability to improve the environment; (2) that these initiatives are likely to encourage protectionism, reduce international trade, and hence slow the recovery of the U.S. and world economies; and (3) that slower growth will undermine environmental improvements at home and abroad.

Although many environmentalists argue that markets and prosperity are the cause of environmental degradation, our analysis begins with the premise (based on strong evidence) that markets are the source of prosperity and that prosperity and property rights are necessary for environmental quality. If economic growth and international trade are weakened by ill-conceived, risky policies, political support for environmental protection will be reduced, and we may end up with a poorer economy and environment.

Carbon Theory of Value

Given President Obama's focus on climate change, we begin by asking (1) whether the administration's carbon reduction targets are realistic; (2) whether they are likely to have a significant impact on global temperatures in the relevant *political* time frame; (3) what it will cost to achieve these targets; and (4) what regulatory controls (e.g., trade policies) would be necessary to make them effective. We emphasize political time frame because politicians seldom see beyond the next election cycle, while the effects of and solutions to global change require decades.

Without getting into climate science, we stipulate that global temperatures are rising, that some part of the rise is anthropogenic, and that greenhouse gases (GHG) already in the atmosphere will cause temperatures to rise, even if the United States reduces its GHG emissions now. Regardless of the climate model used, it is well accepted that the most realistic targets for reducing current GHG emissions will lower temperatures by only small amounts over the course of the century.

Moreover, trying to set meaningful GHG emission targets is difficult due to the complexities of climate models. As models have been refined to take account of other variables (e.g., ability of oceans to absorb CO_2 and the impact of increased cloud cover associated with CO_2), predicted temperature increases have declined. Also, as models have improved it is clear that climate change will vary considerably from region to region. Due to these complexities, GHG targets are apt to depend as much on politics as they do on science.

In light of this, consider the proposal to stabilize atmospheric

GHG concentrations at 535–550 parts per million (ppm) of CO_2 (about twice the preindustrial level) in an effort to hold global warming to around 2 degrees centigrade (3.6 degrees Fahrenheit) as described in the influential Stern Report. To meet this target, global emissions will have to peak before 2020 and must fall by 2050 to 30 to 60 percent below what they were in 2000. For its part, the Obama administration proposes to reduce U.S. carbon emissions by 14 percent from the 2005 level by 2020 and by 83 percent below the 2005 level by 2050.

Cost estimates for achieving such reductions range between 1 and 3 percent of world gross domestic product (GDP), though the complexities described above make it difficult to get consensus on the cost. Suppose current world GDP grew from its current level of $47 trillion to $94 trillion by 2030 (that is about 3 percent per year) without any emissions reductions. If the cost of achieving targets described above amounts to 3 percent of GDP in 2030, this implies that stabilizing GHG concentrations could cost an average of $117 billion per year in lost economic growth between now and 2030. Just for the United States, the Lieberman-Warner bill under consideration in Congress might cost $800 to $1,300 per household annually by 2015, rising to $1,500 to $2,500 by 2050, according to a study by Charles River Associates. Though some argue that cutting carbon emissions will actually increase GDP through green technologies and green jobs (see discussion below), we think this is unlikely. On the contrary, we believe that the high cost of cutting carbon emissions enough to make any difference in climate will make it difficult for the Obama administration to sell its ambitious agenda to the American public.

Making the sale will be even harder for developing countries where two-thirds to three-fourths of the world's population live. Lifting these populations out of poverty will require formidable increases in the GDP, which will be accompanied by increases in energy use and carbon emissions. Studies predict that global energy demand will increase by 50 percent by 2030, with China and India accounting for approximately 45 percent of the increase. Because most developing economies rely on cheap coal to generate energy (currently nearly 80 percent of China's electricity is provided by coal-fired generation), this growth in demand maps directly into increases in carbon emissions. Given the implications for development, it is not surprising that the leaders of developing countries refuse to join in mandatory, binding GHG discharge targets.

High costs of achieving GHG reductions do not necessarily mean that we should do nothing to mitigate change if the cost of doing nothing is high, and this is precisely what environmentalists argue. The costs of climate change, however, are surprisingly uncertain, despite common rhetoric to the contrary. Except for unanticipated catastrophic effects, most economics studies find small negative global consequences. To be sure, regional impacts of climate change vary, but the aggregate costs are estimated by some to be between 0.08 percent and 0.24 percent of global GDP by the year 2100. Those estimates change periodically, but if the future damage caused by unmitigated climate change is somewhere near these magnitudes and if controlling emissions to stabilize GHG concentrations reduces GDP by 1 to 3 percent, then an aggressive carbon policy does not pass economic muster.

Even if the benefits of pursuing the administration's GHG targets were higher, there is still the question of whether targets can be achieved. Proponents of a cap-and-trade system (see more discussion below) contend that cap-and-trade gets the incentives right for industry to comply (see Fred Krup, *Wall Street Journal*, March 24, 2009). But the World Bank has noted that industry compliance with pollution regulation is far from universal, witness the ineffectiveness of the European Union efforts. If manufacturing facilities migrate offshore in response to higher carbon restrictions in the United States, emissions could rise elsewhere while unemployment and economic stagnation result here at home.

And if achieving compliance in the developed world is a problem, consider what it will be like in countries such as China and

India. Even if their central governments signed on to an international treaty to control global emissions as envisioned by the administration, there is the huge problem of compliance at the local level. In China the hundreds of state-owned enterprises and utilities that generate much of the GHG pollution generally are beyond effective control of the central government. Instead, they are responsive to local party officials whose careers depend on continued economic growth, growth built around cheap, dirty coal. As noted by the Peterson Institute as well as the World Bank, China's administration is far from transparent, even to most Chinese. The problem is replicated in India, Brazil, Indonesia, and so forth.

A final problem with the administration's carbon agenda is that it is likely to be captured by protectionists rather than environmentalists. American unions, already reeling from trade liberalization, are looking for ways to protect their jobs, and so is the administration. Indeed, Energy Secretary Steven Chu called for carbon tariffs as a "weapon" to protect U.S. companies from competition from carbon-intensive imports. As Chu put it, tariffs on imports produced in developing countries lacking tough GHG mandates will help "level the playing field. . . . If other countries don't impose a cost on carbon, then we will be at a disadvantage" (see *Wall Street Journal*, March 18, 2009). With industries such as paper, cement, fertilizer, steel, and glass all facing competition from foreign competition, a tariff in the name of climate change will be welcomed. At a time of a growing sentiment for protectionism (e.g., restrictions on access to U.S. highways by Mexican trucks as part of the North American Free Trade Agreement [NAFTA], "buy America" provisions in the recent stimulus bill, and protective tariffs in Europe and elsewhere), a carbon tariff poses even more fundamental threats to trade.

Administration and measurement costs as well as opportunities to expand tariffs in the name of the environment and GHG controls suggest that the use of trade restrictions as a convenient mechanism to enforce international climate agreements are both naïve, difficult, and dangerous. In a global economy, it is very hard to determine the national origin of final products when components come from many sources and countries, let alone to determine the carbon content and source of products. Any action by the United States to use a carbon tariff is likely to be matched by others, as suggested by China's top climate change negotiator, who said the U.S. proposal to impose import duties on goods from countries that don't try to limit their carbon emissions was "an excuse to impose trade restrictions" under the guise of "climate protection."

It is important to keep in mind that much of the recent global economic growth has been trade-based. When considering protectionism, it is worth remembering the Smoot-Hawley Tariff of 1929 and its damaging impact on world trade, leading to the Great Depression.

All of this suggests that the administration's proposed climate policy will be more costly, will be more damaging to the U.S. and the global economies, and will be less likely to succeed in achieving carbon reduction targets than we have been led to believe. Before undertaking its ambitious climate agenda, the Obama administration should be more transparent with the American public as to the costs and uncertainties of its climate policies and the dangers of an associated trade war. History has shown that societies will bear costs of expensive agendas (e.g., send men to the moon, fight dictators with ambitions for global power) when outcomes are observable and have substantial likely benefits. Unfortunately, in the case climate change, discernible results are very unlikely given the existing concentrations of GHG in the atmosphere and regulatory compliance problems. Couple this with misleading and probably incorrect cost assurances by advocates, the likelihood of a major political backlash is high. Such an outcome surely is not what the administration or supporters of environmental quality have in mind.

An Inconvenient Tax

A possible reaction to these concerns about costs, compliance, and results is that the Obama administration's primary mechanism for reducing carbon emissions—cap-and-trade—will be different. The proposal for capping and reducing carbon emissions in the United States is patterned after the successful SO_2 permit trading system established under the 1990 Clean Air Act Amendments. The right to release carbon is to be limited by the overall cap, and it is a valuable factor of production. Firms holding emission permits can use them as a basis for carbon releases, bank them for future short-falls, or sell to firms that have insufficient permits. In all cases, the permits have value related to the tightness of the cap and the scarcity of permits. By auctioning off the permits, the administration argues that it will capture the value for the public.

For recognizing the potential of a GHG cap-and-trade system to create property rights and thus incentives for reducing emissions, the Obama administration gets high marks. For not recognizing the important differences between applying cap-and-trade to regional SO_2 emissions and to global carbon discharges, and for not recognizing the added costs that auctioning the carbon permits will have on the economy, however, it gets low marks. These costs are in addition to those described above for GHG emission controls.

One of the biggest hurdles to establishing a cap-and-trade system for carbon is allocation of the initial emission permits. In general the Obama administration has followed the lead of the dozens of economists who sent a petition to the House Energy and Commerce Committee on March 3, 2009, calling for auctioning permits, rather than grandfathering them to existing emitters. Economists argue that the revenues raised from auction could be used by the government to reduce distortional income taxes and thereby make the economy more efficient.

If the permits are auctioned, the price paid will become "an inconvient tax" (as it was called by the *Wall Street Journal*, February

27, 2009). And like any other tax, it will be shared by both producers and consumers.

The expected revenue that might be generated from a carbon
permit auction gives some sense of how much this tax will be. The
administration's initial estimates of the expected revenue from a
carbon permit auction were $130–$370 billion annually by 2015
and to total $650 billion over the next ten years. By 2019, auction
revenues will be the sixth-largest source of revenue for the federal
government and may raise as much as $300 billion every year. The
Congressional Budget Office (CBO), however, considers these estimates low and puts the sum closer to $900 billion over the next ten
years. And at a closed meeting on March 17, 2009, administration
officials acknowledged that the auction could raise two to three
times the $650 billion figure (see the *Wall Street Journal*, March 18,
2009).

What ever the number, it is a big pill for producers and consumers to swallow. Moreover, the tax will fall disproportionally on
lower-income families. CBO breaks down the burden of achieving
a 15 percent reduction in carbon emissions as follows: the bottom
quintile of households will see their after-tax income fall by 3.3
percent; the middle quintiles will see theirs fall between 2.7 and 2.9
percent; and the top quintile will see theirs fall by 1.7 percent.

Recognizing the potential for this tax regressivity, the Obama
campaign promised to return the windfall to taxpayers. Now that
he is president, Obama wants $525 billion to go, through its "mak-
ing work pay" tax credit, to taxpayers who do not pay income taxes.
This amounts to $400 for individuals and $800 for families earning
less than $250,000 per year. The president's budget further pro-
poses to use another $120 billion to fund clean energy technology.

Any realistic political analysis, however, raises questions about
the likelihood that the auction revenues will be redistributed to the
public. Already, the administration is on the defensive and strapped
for cash to fund its policy objectives. In March the CBO's baseline
projections of the budget deficit for 2009 and 2010 rose, leading to

estimates that the deficit will total $1.7 trillion, or 11.9 percent of GDP, this year, the largest since 1945, when World War II ended. Accordingly, the opportunity to use cap-and-trade auctions as a revenue source becomes overwhelmingly appealing, potentially hijacking the environment objectives. Further, with windfall tax revenues such as these, political scientists predict that a disproportionate amount of the revenues are likely to go to special-interest groups, with the amount determined largely by lobbying effort.

Lest you be skeptical that auction revenues will go to uses other than tax refunds, consider what happened to tobacco settlement revenues. In November 1998 a settlement was reached between the major U.S. tobacco producers and forty-six states. In exchange for dropping their lawsuits, states were to receive payments from the tobacco companies projected to be $206 billion over the first twenty-five years. These payments were to be used for the advancement of public health and the implementation of tobacco-related health measures. To date, $79.2 billion from tobacco settlement money has been received by the states. Between 2000 and 2005, 30 percent of the money went to health-related spending, but the rest went to everything from infrastructure to public debt service, the latter of which took 5.4 percent of the revenues.

The Adaptation Strategy

Though cap-and-trade is a property rights approach to environmental problems that has been successfully applied to regional fisheries and SO_2 controls, it is not as efficacious for global carbon emission controls because of uncertainties regarding costs and benefits and worldwide compliance. Given the stipulation that we are experiencing global warming and that it might lead to possible catastrophic events, if not cap-and-trade, then what?

To get at the answer, put the issue in the context of risk analysis. Some policy analysts contend that incurring the huge costs of reducing carbon is like buying insurance. But unlike insurance which pools risk and pays those insured if and when they have a loss, spending money now to potentially avoid uncertain future costs has no such pooling benefit. Instead of being like fire insurance, it is more like buying a smoke detector. As such, the decision to reduce the likelihood of a catastrophic event depends on the cost of prevention versus the expected cost of the event. Because the smoke detector is cheap relative to a bad fire, almost all homes have them. Based on the cost-benefit evidence of reducing CO_2 emissions, however, it appears that rather than reducing risk, the administration's policies could increase it. They could make the United States and the world poorer and, therefore, not only less able to respond to climate change but also more vulnerable to other threats, such as terrorism and general unrest as the world's populations see constrained opportunities and dashed expectations. We recognize that there are potential costs to climate change, but at this time, an aggressive emissions control policy through cap-and-trade is apt to be counterproductive economically, politically, and environmentally (i.e., have little real impact on global temperatures in the foreseeable future).

Fortunately, there are policies that will help to more effectively adapt to global warming. For example, state insurance regulators are requiring that insurance companies disclose the added risk that they are likely to face if warming occurs. Such disclosure provides better information of the expected cost of global warming and therefore a price signal to reduce that cost just as do higher fire insurance rates. Encouraging the provision of transparent information is something the Obama administration should consider.

Similarly, as the administration considers subsidies such as those to agriculture, it should ask whether subsidies encourage or discourage adaptation to climate-related events. Subsidizing flood, hurricane, and crop insurance is exactly the wrong thing to do in the face of global warming because such subsidies create a moral hazard problem. Subsidies to corn-based ethanol production are now widely recognized as detrimental to the land on which corn is grown and as having little, no, or perhaps even a detrimental effect on GHG emissions.

Land prices are another signal that will help us adapt. Some of France's wine production is moving to Germany as vintners antici-pate better climates for grapes further north. Land trusts, such as the Nature Conservancy, which seek to preserve habitat for endan-gered species through conservation easements, are beginning to ask whether they should anticipate where the environment needs to be conserved rather than reacting to past changes.

Climate change predictably will have a big impact on the timing and distribution of precipitation. For the western United States, climate models generally indicate that higher global temperatures will lead to shifts in the timing and location of precipitation, rather than reductions in overall precipitation. This may require more freshwater storage dams and distribution canals. Preparation for such changes ought to be given priority.

Furthermore, water markets can generate information about rel-ative values and encourage more efficient water use. They can alle-viate the need for expensive, energy-consuming desalinization projects and reduce reliance on costly, controversial, and often inef-fective water rationing by government. Water markets, however, require more precise definition of and commitment to water rights, and streamlined regulatory processes to lower the costs of water transactions. This includes making it possible for water trades across political boundaries, which could be accomplished under interstate water compacts. Although states are a focal point for much of what needs to happen to facilitate water markets, the fed-eral government can be influential, especially in regions where it supplies a large share of the water.

The Obama administration's green jobs agenda could fit into an adaptation strategy if it would establish transparent strategies for identifying which jobs are worth encouraging for reducing GHG emissions. Because of the overriding incentives to use coal in the developing world, new methods of reducing its carbon releases could have an important payoff. This does not mean throwing money at any alternative energy development. Rather, it means doing what government can do well, namely, focus on basic research. This is where America has led the world in the past and where it can continue to do so.

GREEN JOBS THEORY OF VALUE

President Obama has made green job creation a central part of both his environmental and his stimulus policies. And who could be opposed to such a policy, given that green means good for the environment and that jobs are seen as the way of getting the economy out of the doldrums? We ask here whether appearance is reality.

Is Green Really Green?

At a time when everything, from produce to household cleaners to radio stations, claims to be green, it is not surprising that politicians would jump on the "greener than thou" bandwagon (see Anderson and Huggins's book by that title from the Hoover Institution Press, 2008). Defining what is green, however, is not easy.

The administration's definition of green jobs seems to center around industry categories rather than measures of environmental quality. Hence, jobs from generating electricity from renewable sources, from producing ethanol, or from constructing energy saving buildings are all considered green. Ethanol stands out in this list, given that, "instead of producing a 0 percent savings [of carbon dioxide], [it] nearly doubles greenhouse emissions over 30 years" (see Timothy Searchinger et al., *Science*, 2008).

Hence, we must ask whether simply asserting jobs to be green is sufficient. If the administration really wants to improve the environment with a jobs policy, it will have to undertake more precise, transparent calculations to determine what constitutes green. In the absence of precision and transparency, special interests are likely to make the case for subsidizing their jobs, regardless of how good they might be for the environment.

Are Green Jobs Better?

Just as the administration is asking us to take it on faith that green is green, it is asking us to take it on faith that green jobs are better for the economy. Accepting this requires several heroic assumptions, which are covered in much more detail in a study entitled "The Methodologies of Green Jobs," by Andrew P. Morriss, William T. Bogart, Andrew Dorchak, and Roger E. Meiners, released on March 26, 2009, by the Institute for Energy Research. The following is a summary of their arguments.

1. *Green jobs produce goods and services that are more valuable than the cost of production.* Profitable markets require that revenue or product value exceed production costs, but politically mandated job creation does not. The fact that green jobs must be subsidized suggests that such jobs have not passed this market test either because the cost of production is too high, the value of what is produced is too low, or both. Just as spending money on carbon reduction may not be worth it because we are unlikely to get much temperature reduction, spending money on green jobs is not worth it if added GDP from green jobs could be gotten for less money in other sectors. To be sure there are subsidies all over the economy, especially in energy, but the amount of the subsidies increases with "greenness." For example, the average subsidy per megawatt hour (Mwh) of electricity produced from coal is $0.44 compared to $2.80 per Mwh from renewable energy sources. Studies of other government job-creation programs show that between 10 and 60 percent of the jobs created by subsidies would not have existed if left to the marketplace.

2. *A green job is a net addition to employment.* Estimates of the number of jobs created by green government spending ignore the potential crowding-out effect. The proper measure would be net new jobs created rather than green jobs created where the money is spent. Consider whether a job in the renewable energy sector reduces unemployment. If that energy crowds out a job in a fossil fuel plant, the net effect on employment will be zero. There are no good data for saying what this crowding-out effect is with green jobs, but there are plenty of studies for other sectors such as construction of sports stadiums, higher education, and industrial plant location. All reach the conclusion that the crowding-out effect is not zero.

3. *Substituting labor for capital increases productivity.* Green jobs typically mean substituting labor for capital or other inputs. For example, a job in recycling labor is a substitute for sand in the case of glass or growing trees in the case of paper. Economists generally agree that substituting labor for capital reduces labor productivity and thus lowers labor wages. Indeed, most of the growth in wages in the twentieth and twenty-first centuries in the United States and elsewhere has been through increases in capital per worker and new technologies. This is precisely what Karl Marx missed with his "labor theory of value," and what the administration is missing with a green jobs policy.

4. *Spending tax money on green jobs has a low or no opportunity cost.* In fact, United Nations Environment Programme goes even one better, claiming that green jobs pay a "double dividend" in the form of jobs and environmental quality. The opportunity cost question is obviously closely related to net job creation but is broader in that it asks what might happen if green job money were spent elsewhere. A quick look at numbers suggests that green jobs are expensive. A study by the Carbon Action Partnership estimated that $100 billion invested in green job creation would yield 935,200 jobs. That number sounds good until one realizes that this is a cost of $107,000 per job. Could this sum be better spent on health care

to save lives or college education to increase human capital? Once the size of these opportunity costs becomes evident, expect green fur to fly.

Greening of the Marketplace

The caveats just raised about green job creation do not mean that green jobs will not drive a portion of our economy's future. In fact, the American Solar Energy Society claims that there were 8.5 million jobs in the alternative energy and energy efficiency sectors in 2006 and that there will be 16.3 million such jobs by 2030 without the new policies favored by the Obama administration. Although we can not be sure of the accuracy of these claims or of how many such jobs resulted from the helping hand of government subsidies, we can be sure that the green sector will continue via the invisible hand of the marketplace.

As with global warming, the lesson key for the Obama administration is to let market prices reflect resource scarcity and provide incentives for private investment that are profitable and therefore sustainable. The viability of this approach is illustrated by what the marketplace did for energy efficiency between 1970 and 2000. In 1970 experts warned that growing demands for energy would cause us to run out of supplies by the end of the century. We know today, however, that demand predictions were 60 to 80 percent too high, mainly because energy savings stimulated mostly by the market caused energy use per dollar of GDP to fall by 36 percent.

Green Protectionism

As taxpayer money is distributed across the country to advance energy independence and to create green jobs, what happens if solar panels and windmill blades are more efficiently made elsewhere, say in Mexico or China? It is easy to imagine the outcry of politicians when solar power firms or wind energy generators, who have received subsidies, seek to buy imported turbines or panels. There is no reason to expect that the United States will have a comparative advantage in this type of production. Indeed, once the technology is made routine, these inputs will be commodities that are likely to be produced in low-cost labor markets. This is a good outcome for alternative energy entrepreneurs who seek to profit from producing low-cost alternative energy. But it is not apt to be favored by unions or politicians. Again, the specter of environmental tariffs emerges. The inclination to resort to trade restrictions seems unavoidable. Yet, trade restrictions can only make all of us and our environment poorer. Our advantage is in technology, not in basic production. The administration should be up-front about this.

A Healthy Economy Means a Healthy Environment

The Obama administration's concern about the environment is laudable. Its concern about the economy and the welfare of the country's population also is laudable. These objectives are interwoven. The U.S. and world economies cannot be saddled with high costs, trade barriers, and policies that are likely to have little environmental benefit. Environmental gains are most possible when societies are prosperous and flexible. Despite the pressures from many sectors to rush forward with an aggressive carbon reduction agenda, this is not the time to do so. Candor as to what is known, what is and is not possible, and what trade-offs are likely to be encountered will be more effective in securing political support for devising long-term environmental policies for adaptation and mitigation than any hastily assembled environmental package based on a cap-and-trade system for carbon and green jobs.

6 What's Wrong with the Employee Free Choice Act?

Richard A. Epstein

T he first one hundred days of the Obama administration have been marked by its determination to pass the revolutionary Employee Free Choice Act (EFCA), which was introduced in Congress on March 10, 2009. As of this writing, it looks as though the bill will not pass this year, given the unanimous Republican opposition to it in the Senate. But the issue is likely to be revived again during the Obama presidency, as it has been before, so it is important to examine its provisions because it raises important issues of principle. In addition, it has gathered an impressive level of political and intellectual support. In particular, the EFCA has received the endorsement of the Democratic National Convention Platform Committee of prominent economists, under the aegis of the Economic Policy Institute, and of President Obama and Vice President Biden. In a recent congressional hearing before the 110th Congress on February 8, the EFCA was defended as the means to return to the management-labor balance under the National Labor Relations Act of 1935 (the NLRA, in its original form is commonly referred to as the Wagner Act), said to be the surest way to revive the fortunes of a shrinking middle class.

The reality, however, is otherwise. The EFCA would hamper the efficiency of labor markets in ways that make the road to economic recovery far steeper than necessary. Generally, it will severely hurt the very persons whom it intends to help. Dire consequences of this sort do not occur by happenstance. They are driven by a misconceived vision that strengthening union monopolies will improve the overall operation of labor markets. But monopolies are as socially unwise in labor markets as they are everywhere else. Shrinking the size of the social pie hurts many in the short run and benefits no one in the long run. Wages and productivity are inextricably linked in the economy as a whole. The central mission of sound labor policy is to grow the economic pie to create greater opportunities for all. Employers should not be demonized; workers should not be canonized. We want firms and workers to make the best deals for themselves by playing within the rules of the game. The key task of labor policy is to determine how to best structure those rules.

Accordingly, part I of this chapter outlines the proper role for freedom of contract in organizing labor markets. Part II compares this vision with the modern collective bargaining regime under the NLRA as it is currently organized. Part III explains the overall decline in labor unions over the past fifty years. Part IV explores how the key provisions of the EFCA will further deteriorate our overall economic conditions, followed by a brief conclusion.

How Labor Markets Work

Labor contracts are governed by the same principles applicable to all exchange relationships. Any voluntary exchange (i.e., one not tainted with force or fraud) generates social improvement. First, the exchange produces mutual gain between the parties. Self-interested people make deals only when they value what they receive more than what they surrender and find their trading partners by voluntary choice, not by government decree. A strong legal system enforces each deal in accordance with its express provisions. Judges do not impose their own visions of a just contractual order on the parties, who are free to adopt whatever business arrangements they see fit. Keeping transaction costs low allows for the rapid deployment and redeployment of labor. Savvy contracting parties use the outputs from one agreement as inputs for the next. Over time, sophisticated parties build up complex supply and distribution chains, which bring more goods to market at lower prices.

These myriad developments also benefit outsiders by expanding their business opportunities. One vital exception, however, does not, properly speaking, involve an exchange of goods or service at all, but rather concerns "horizontal" agreements between individuals or firms on the *same* side of the market to restrict output and raise prices. These cartel-like arrangements, of course, reduce overall social welfare by cutting back output and raising prices. Their externalities are systematically *negative*.

Critics of labor markets claim that these arrangements aren't truly competitive because employers and employees don't routinely dicker over contract terms. They view take-it-or-leave-it offers as signs of private coercion. Unfortunately, this common claim ignores the insight that efficient markets increase the number of transactions completed relative to the transaction costs of completing them. Any dickering between two neighbors over the backyard fence is a sign of a "thin" market with only a few participants, slowing down deal creation. In contrast, "thick" markets, with lots of buyers and sellers, employers and employees, operate more quickly and quietly. Knowledgeable actors on both sides of the market gravitate quickly to a competitive price or wage that less-knowledgeable participants then use as guides for their own dealings. Speedy negotiations are a sign of active competition, not decrepit markets. With time, unregulated markets incorporate technological improvements, which in turn lead to a rise in real wages, a decline in child labor, a reduction in working hours, and an increase in life expectancy—largely without government intervention. This was the outcome during the relative open market policies of the first third of the twentieth century.

The Current Labor Law Synthesis

The rejection of competitive markets shaped the New Deal legislation of the 1930s. The progression from competition to state monopoly proceeded as follows. In 1914, section Six of the Clayton Act exempts voluntary agreements among workers from the operation of the antitrust laws:

> The labor of a human being is not a commodity or article of commerce. Nothing contained in the antitrust laws shall be construed to forbid the existence and operation of labor, agricultural, or horticultural organizations, instituted for the purposes of mutual help, and not having capital stock or conducted for profit, or to forbid or restrain individual members of such organizations from lawfully carrying out the legitimate objects thereof; nor shall such organizations, or the members thereof, be held or construed to be illegal combinations or conspiracies in restraint of trade, under the antitrust laws.

But, in and of itself, that statutory advantage could not guarantee the widespread penetration of labor unions into American industries. Employers could still reach out to third persons and refuse to bargain with any union.

The 1935 version of the NLRA plugged both these chinks in the union's armor. First, it allowed workers to decide by majority vote in secret-ballot elections whether or not to appoint a union representative as their exclusive bargaining agent. The act contemplated an extensive and vigorous democratic campaign that let all interested parties have their say before the vote was taken. Once the union prevailed by majority vote, however, it gained the exclusive statutory right to bargain for all workers. Employers were prohibited from having any direct contact with individual workers as long as the union was in place, and the collective bargaining agreement displaced all preexisting contracts.

Second, the NLRA has always required the parties to bargain in

good faith with an eye to making an agreement; refusals to negotiate were branded unfair labor practices (ULPs). The statutory
good-faith standard was meant to block the employer from stone-
walling the union after its certification. But the meaning of good
faith remains elusive more than seventy years after the passage of
the statute. Good faith does not require either side to make concessions; good faith does not refer to honesty in business dealings.
Rather, its key components are that the employer must disclose key
information to enable the union to better formulate its demands
and must not make offers directly to workers that undercut the role
of the union as the designated bargaining agent.

The economic case made for the NLRA also rests on false premises. The first is that unequal bargaining positions between labor
and employers preclude "actual liberty of contract," according to
the NLRA statement of findings. But inequality of bargaining power
is a phrase devoid of descriptive content. Any employer who pos-
sessed that advantage would drive its hapless workers, regardless of
skill levels, down to the minimum wage. That doesn't happen
because workers can sell their services to other firms that will bid
wages up to a competitive level. The relative revenues or net worth
of firms and workers do not set the equilibrium wage. The number
of choices available to employers or employees does.

The NLRA is also defended on the ground that higher union
wages increase the purchasing power of workers in ways that jump-
start the overall economy—the precise argument that the Obama
team uses to support the EFCA. But it does not work. The workers
who receive higher wages do have greater purchasing power, but
nonunion workers who are pushed aside have less purchasing
power. Additionally, higher prices for consumer goods diminish
purchasing power, even for union members. In short, overall social
welfare is not improved by moving further away from a competitive
equilibrium.

Most critically, in practice the effects of the NLRA are uniformly
counterproductive. Its novel institutional arrangements invert the

relationship between transaction costs and completed transactions. Its monopoly bargaining regime creates a wide range of possible outcomes for any negotiation, not only on wages but on all other mandatory terms of negotiation: pensions, benefits, grievances, promotions, and the like. Each party has an incentive to hold out for a large fraction of the gap between the competitive and the monopoly wage. Management and labor gird for titanic battles that may end in employer lockouts or worker strikes, both of which disrupt key relationships with customers and suppliers. Permanent replacements, even though available in some instances under current law, offer an imperfect mitigation device.

In the short run, this complex administrative structure can at times produce gains for some unionized workers. But, on a sustained basis, the NLRA's confrontational approach is incapable of developing a thriving middle class, as is commonly claimed by labor supporters. In fact, it is just as likely to take small employers out of the middle class as it is to push poorer workers into it. The current legal regime entrenches two key sources of social loss: monopolistic structures coupled with high administrative, compliance, and bargaining costs. Neither can we overlook the personal casualties under the NLRA. Currently, millions of individuals have lost their jobs because unions overplayed their hands in collective bargaining negotiations; the shuttered GM factories offer mute testimony to the risks of aggressive bargaining strategies.

THE DECLINE OF UNIONIZATION

Much of the push for the EFCA is a result of the decline in union membership over the years, notwithstanding the extraordinary protections that labor unions receive under the NLRA. For its first two decades, the NLRA generated a steep increase in unionization levels; the next half century, however, saw a slow and steady decline of private unions. From a peak of about 35 percent of workers in unions in1955, today unions only represent about 8 percent.

Why this decline? Union leaders adamantly insist that the current rules are stacked against their organization efforts, including bitter employer opposition to unionization efforts. Those campaigns are, however, a result of the complex NLRA bargaining framework, which substitutes divisive politics for unanimous agreement by firms and workers. To obtain the critical votes needed under a regime of majority rule, both sides work overtime to attract members to their side. Which side has the advantage under current rules is uncertain. Today, the NLRA allows employers to make statements that predict the economic dislocations that will ensue if the union prevails; it also bans both threats of retaliation and promises of benefits to workers who steer clear of union membership. But it does not prevent employers, at their own expense, from holding mandatory sessions to explain their views. The union, on the other hand, faces no such constraints on either promises or threats and can approach workers in unsupervised settings. The union can also decide when to launch its campaign and when to ask for an election. It is not uncommon for unions to delay an election to turn up the pressure with pickets and publicity campaigns, as was seen in the case between the Service Employees International Union (SEIU) and the MGM Grand Hotel (which may now file for bankruptcy). The SEIU's prolonged campaign relied on pickets and other public relations tools to organize the Las Vegas hotel. By refusing to ask for an immediate election, the union was able to force the management to accept a card-check determination, allowing it to gain recognition by getting cards from just over 52 percent of the unit members. And it actively sought so-called neutrality agreements that require the employer to stand silently aside while the union gathers cards that generate union recognition without a secret-ballot election.

However one weighs the pros and cons, the point is that these election rules have undergone no substantial changes during the past fifty years. Similarly, union claims of an increased rate of employer ULPs rest on shaky empirical data. The current number of employer ULP charges filed does not reflect any increase, given that these charges are often dismissed or abandoned, and more reliable evidence suggests fewer ULPs filed by employer. Today, most organization campaigns tend to be fought to a draw, with unions and employers having about equal fortunes in NLRB-supervised elections.

Thus, the explanation for union decline must lie elsewhere. One possibility is the increased sophistication of employers' defensive strategies, but these are matched by equally greater sophistication on the union side. In fact, the factors appear to be clearly structural. The assembly line of 1940 has given way to more-complex organizational arrangements in which workers assume more-specialized roles. No single union message can appeal to all workers; educated workers, for example, realize that the union cannot negotiate an overall agreement that will accurately reflect their diverse positions. Higher job turnover also makes it hard to persuade workers who may change jobs tomorrow to form a union today. In addition, in many manufacturing and service industries, the reduction of trade barriers reduces the monopoly rents that firms can extract in a given product market, which also makes it more difficult for unions to extract wage premiums in highly competitive markets. Finally, much of the decline in union membership is attributable not to sputtering organizational drives but to mass attrition in key industries, such as automobiles and steel, where declining market share has led to mass layoffs, in part because manifest wage rigidity in labor contracts prevents the needed downward adjustment in wages and benefits. Bilateral renegotiation, however, is both too little and too late.

THE EMPLOYEE FREE CHOICE ACT

The flawed economic analysis of the pro-union advocates undermines their case for the EFCA. Reduced output cannot jump-start production or propel more workers into the middle class; vague appeals to "balance" cannot remove the dysfunctional features of mandatory collective bargaining. Even an efficient monopolist reduces labor supply and increases costs, resulting in social losses. A recent study by Anne Layne-Farrar of LECG quantifies the relationship between increased union penetration into the workforce and increased levels of unemployment. Her study estimates that every 1.0 percent increase in unionization rates leads to a 0.30 to 0.35 percent increase in the level of unemployment. Union leaders boast that they can increase union membership in the private sector by more than one million a year. A 5 percent increase in union membership in a workforce of 150 million people, therefore, cashes out, over a five-year period, to a loss of about two and a quarter million jobs.

Indeed, the situation is even worse. Labor unions are inefficient monopolists that must insist on Byzantine work rules to share the wealth among union members so as to maintain their critical level of worker support. In looking out for their members (and for their leadership), unions have every incentive to ignore the opportunities for advancement lost by nonunion workers. The picture is not rosy. The EFCA's three key provisions, still very much on the table, give still more reason for pessimism:

1. *Extra Sanctions for Employers' Organizational Activities.* The first, and most modest, change in the EFCA toughens sanctions against employers that the National Labor Relations Board (NLRB) finds have committed ULPs during union organizational drives. Back-pay awards are trebled, and employers can be subject to fines of up to $20,000 per violation (the scope of such violations is left undefined). But multiple violations are likely in prolonged and bitter campaigns. In addition, investigating the ULPs takes priority over all other NLRB activities, with no corresponding priority for dealing with union ULPs or increases in penalties for unions. That provision makes it more costly for employers to mount a defense to a unionization campaign, which in turn emboldens union

organizational behavior. In the end, this provision will most likely modestly increase union membership and the consequent social dislocations.

2. *The Card Check.* The ECFA's first major innovation authorizes the use of a card check as a substitute for secret-ballot elections. Although some union supporters note that the secret-ballot election is still "available" under the new statute, that is only a play on words. The relevant statutory provision, in the proposed *Employee Free Choice Act of 2009*, reads in full:

> [W]henever a petition shall have been filed by an employee or group of employees or any individual or labor organization acting in their behalf alleging that a majority of employees in a unit appropriate for the purposes of collective bargaining wish to be represented by an individual or labor organization for such purposes, the Board shall investigate the petition.

Essentially, then, it takes only one employee, represented by any union, to initiate the card-check process. The secret-ballot option, however, remains available only when the union wants it, which is basically never.

This provision quoted above transforms the process of unionization. The current rules let unions use cards signed by 30 percent of the workers to trigger a secret-ballot election. In practice, most unions only move forward if they collect signed cards from a clear majority of workers, knowing that some workers sign cards to fend off pressure and others change their minds after they hear both sides. The secret-ballot election, then, allows all workers to voice their preferences without being under the watchful eye of *either* side.

The EFCA removes the secret-ballot buffer that now stands between the union and the worker by allowing unions to collect cards *in secret* so as to get a leg up in the card-check derby before either the employer or the dissident workers can respond. In some small businesses, employers may not learn of the campaign until the union has been certified by the NLRB. The cards need not be notarized to be valid nor must the union return the cards to any worker who requests them. Challenges to the signed cards are allowed on only the narrowest of grounds (forgery) but not on grounds of union coercion or misrepresentation. Indeed, every Republican proposal to limit union discretion in running card checks was uniformly rejected by Democrats in committee during the 110th Congress.

This loaded procedure is not just a departure from the ordinary rules of voluntary agreement but also a stunning repudiation of the central premise of the NLRA: that a democratic process should decide whether or not a union will represent workers. The EFCA undermines the right of all workers to participate in a deliberative process concerning the decision of whether or not to accept a union. Imagine Congress enacting laws when half of its members had signed a bill but before there was any opportunity for debate! I believe that this truncation of the deliberative process violates constitutional guarantees associated with free speech and due process of law, as I wrote in an article entitled "The Ominous Employee Free Choice Act" (Regulation, spring 2009). In any event, these rules represent horrible policy. Unions have long supported the aptly named Worker Adjustment and Retraining Notification Act (WARN), which, roughly speaking, requires employers to give sixty days notice before closing any plant or facility with more than one hundred workers. If unions believe notice is justified here, why do they oppose a simple limitation that would make cards valid only if they are signed and notarized after a public announcement is made that the campaign has begun?

3. *Compulsory Interest Arbitration.* Arbitration has had a long and honorable place in helping resolve grievances that arise under preexisting collective bargaining agreements. But grievance arbitration only works because the NLRA requires the parties to bargain in good faith to reach an agreement. In its most radical provision,

however, the EFCA introduces a regime of mandatory interest arbitration that has never been used before in the private sector. Under the EFCA, an arbitration board would be charged with designing the basic contract from top to bottom, starting with a blank piece of paper. Although public unions often arbitrate under similar schemes, which are also imposed on local governments by state legislatures, the EFCA proposes extending this practice into the private sector. Compulsory interest arbitrations can help avoid strikes that might otherwise disrupt vital services. But as the years pass, these agreements will introduce a degree of structural rigidity that will make it impossible to reorganize any unionized activity. The longer the basic template remains in place, the less well it works. Unions can also use their political clout with legislators to increase pension obligations whose cumulative impact has led to large budgets deficits in such key states as California and New York.

Mandatory interest arbitration will work far worse under the EFCA, which offers zero guidance on how its ambitious arbitration system will operate. It does, however, set up an impossible timetable that requires negotiations to start within ten days of union recognition, even for employers who have received no prior notice. Next, it allows only ninety days for unaided negotiations to run their course; thereafter, a mediator has thirty days to help the parties reach an agreement before the case is designated for compulsory interest arbitration. Beyond this bare timetable, the EFCA offers no hint as to what adjustments should be made in the schedule if the process is derailed. If the mediator is not available on the ninety-first day, no one knows whether the thirty-day period is suspended or continues to run. And although the supposed timetables are strict up to the arbitral phase, the EFCA does not specify how long it will take to convene an arbitration panel, how that will be done, how long the panel will gather evidence, or when it will issue a so-called first contract, which then lasts two years. The original mandated arrangement could easily run hundreds of pages of text and appendixes addressing the full range of mandatory bargaining topics, which include wages, pensions, fringe benefits, absences, overtime, demotions, grievances, contracting out, and countless more. Neither is it clear whether that decree takes effect only when issued or whether it relates back to the time of union recognition or just to the start of arbitration. How businesses are supposed to fly blind in the transitional period is never explained.

More frighteningly, the EFCA gives neither the union nor the employer any say as of right in the choice of the members of the arbitration board. The entire provision reads:

> The [Federal Mediation and Conciliation] Service shall refer the dispute to an arbitration board established in accordance with such regulations as may be prescribed by the Service. The arbitration panel shall render a decision settling the dispute and such decision shall be binding upon the parties for a period of 2 years, unless amended during such period by written consent of the parties.

As a matter of principle, this provision of the EFCA wholly repudiates the central premise of the original NLRA as stated by the Senate Committee on Education and Labor:

> The committee wishes to dispel any possible false impression that this bill is designed to compel the making of agreements or to permit governmental supervision of their terms. It must be stressed that the duty to bargain collectively does not carry with it the duty to reach an agreement, because the essence of collective bargaining is that either party shall be free to decide whether proposals made to it are satisfactory.

The EFCA then goes on to implement its novel program in the worst possible way. The statute supplies no blueprint for the selection of arbitrators but entrusts that decision to a partisan political figure, the chair of the Federal Mediation and Conciliation Service

(FMCS), appointed by the secretary of labor. In the Obama admin-istration, in that cabinet office is Hilda Solis, meaning that the appointed FMCS chair is certain to be sympathetic to the union side. Also, nothing prevents the FMCS from making all arbitrators full-time employees of the FMCS or limits the ability of the FMCS to designate its own list of arbitrators from whom the parties must choose. No substantive standards limit the discretion of the arbitra-tion board, whose determinations could destroy the business model of many firms, impair their profitability, or force them to slash workforces or close divisions. And if these are forbidden under the initial arbitration decree, nothing can forestall the inevitable plunge into bankruptcy.

The burdens on the nascent arbitration system are extraordinary because large retailers and chains could face many simultaneous arbitrations. Yet nothing in the EFCA coordinates the decisions of the multiple arbitration boards that might have to deal with sepa-rate units within a large integrated firm. Indeed, one likely shortcut is that arbitration boards will take existing union contracts and impose them by decree on formerly nonunion businesses, which could help cartelize labor markets through government interven-tion. Furthermore, nothing in the EFCA ensures that these numer-ous decrees will not be riddled with inconsistencies and ambiguities that could take weeks or months to iron out. The EFCA also makes the arbitration decision "final," which precludes the possibility of any judicial appeal. Throughout it all, the repre-sented workers have no collective say in the selection of the union or in the ratification of the supposed contract. The entire process reads like a partial nationalization of every firm subject to the EFCA's reach. And if today the EFCA governs for two years, a stroke of the congressional pen could extend it time and again—to give the scheme time to prove itself, of course. How this ill-con-ceived system of state coercion and expropriation is supposed to create jobs is a mystery. How this system could survive a constitu-tional challenge is every bit as mysterious when biased arbitration panels can force parties to enter into losing deals. If the government cannot force me to pay $250,000 for a house that is worth $100,000, how can it force me to hire labor for what I think is worth one hundred dollars an hour for only forty dollars? The NLRA lets an employer walk away from a losing deal; the EFCA forces the firm to eat its losses.

A GRIM CONCLUSION

It is a sad sign of the temper of the times that so destructive a statute attracted so much political support before faltering. I do not wish to defend the current system from its critics (of whom I am one) who prefer a competitive employment market. Any process whereby unions are selected by majority vote comes out a distinct second to market institutions that operate under a principle of unanimous consent. It is therefore no surprise that no one is happy with the current configuration of the NLRA. But for all its manifest flaws, the current system is light years ahead of the EFCA. The central choice that faces any political system is whether it wants its productive processes to be organized by state coercion or voluntary association. State coercion is vulnerable to massive interference by public officials and outright capture by well-situated interest groups. Voluntary association allows parties to harness their private knowledge to improve their market positions through gains from trade. The current system lies midway between the two poles. The EFCA pushes the system decidedly to the authoritarian pole and, in so doing, mocks the principle of free choice that it claims to embrace. It denies choices to dissident workers when unions are formed and union contracts ratified. It puts employers, without their consent, under the thumb of government administrators. Beyond their posturing, the EFCA's advocates have offered no explanation of how the heavy hand of government can increase productivity or improve labor relations. Union bosses and government bureaucrats gain from this system. Everyone else loses.

REFERENCES

The Democratic National Convention Committee, "The Democratic National Platform: Renewing America's Promise," (2008): 14–15, http://www.democrats.org/a/party/platform.html.

Economic Policy Institute, "Prominent Economists Say: Passage of the Employee Free Choice Act is Critical to Rebuilding our Economy and Strengthening our Democracy," http://epi.3cdn.net/1eb9aba51935a 5b82b_13m6iixpt.pdf.

Strengthening America's Middle Class through the Employee Free Choice Act: Hearing on H.R. 800 before the Subcomm. on Health, Employment, Labor, and Pensions, 110th Cong., 1st sess., at 4. (February 8, 2007).

Richard A. Epstein, *How Progressives Rewrote the Constitution* (Washington, D.C.: The Cato Institute, 2006).

Richard A. Epstein, The Ominous Employee Free Choice Act, Regulation 48 (Spring 2009).

Clayton Antitrust Act, Section Six, Code 15 (1914), § 17.

J.I. Case Co. v. NLRB, 321 U.S. 332 (1944).

Anne Layne-Farrar, "An Empirical Assessment of the Employee Free Choice Act: The Economic Implications," http://ssrn.com/abstract = 1353305.

Minority Views, Report on the Employee Free Choice Act of 2007 (H.R. 800), 110th Cong., 1st sess., H.R. Rep. 110–23, at 58–59 (2007).

Worker Adjustment and Retraining Notification Act, U.S. Code 29 (1989),§§ 2101 et seq.

Employee Free Choice Act of 2007, H.R. 800, 110th Cong., 1st sess., (February 5, 2007), § 3.

S. Rep. No. 74–573, 74th Cong., 1st sess., 12 (1935), *reprinted in* National Labor Relations Board, *Legislative History of the* National Labor Relations Act *of 1935,* 2d. ed. (Washington, D.C.: U.S. Govt. Print. Off., 1985).

7   Health Care One More Time

Richard A. Epstein

P eople on all sides of the political spectrum agree that the crazy-quilt of the American health-care system needs major revamping. The analysis typically revolves around three interrelated axes: access, cost, and quality.

On access, the dominant concern is the forty-six million individuals who do not have health insurance, plus those who may lose their coverage if the current recession deepens. That figure is, however, subject to important refinements: about ten million of those who are uninsured have had to opt out of the market because of high prices; about twelve million are eligible for government programs in which they have not enrolled; about 4.1 million children are now eligible for inclusion in the expanded State Children's Health Insurance Program (SCHIP); and another ten million are illegal immigrants. The remaining fourteen million represent less than 5 percent of the overall population. Any comprehensive health-care plan must at a minimum address each of these groups.

On cost, health care now gobbles up an ever larger fraction of gross domestic product (GDP). Three numbers capture the overall picture. First, total health-care expenditures reached $2.4 trillion in 2007, almost 17 percent of GDP, or about $7,900 per person. The projections are for more of the same. One estimate has 17.6 percent of GDP going for health care in the year 2009 (see http://homecare

mag.com/news/health-care-spending-exceed-gdp-growth-20090224).
Another estimate finds that $4.3 trillion, or 20 percent of GDP, will
be spent on health care as of 2017 (see www.nchc.org/facts/cost
.shtml). Poorer countries have lower costs, broader health-care coverage, and longer life expectancies. What, if anything, would allow
us to spend health-care dollars more efficiently than we do today?

On quality, at its best American health-care is as good as or better than any other throughout the world. But U.S. quality standards
are far from uniform, and the uneasy sense is that the insistent cost
pressures on the system will erode health-care quality in ways hard
to identify and harder to correct. How should we cut this Gordian
knot?

The first hundred days of the Obama term have yielded only
hints as to its eventual approach because the going is necessarily
slow. Health-care reform is more complex than labor market
reform, which has generated a huge hubbub involving the (mis-
named) Employee Free Choice Act, legislation that is only two
pages long. No one can pack health-care reform into that small a
nutshell. In addition, the Obama team lost momentum when former Senate majority leader Tom Daschle, a consummate insider,
was forced to withdraw his nomination for secretary of health and
human services, paving the way for former Kansas governor Kath-
leen Sebelius, who is not. As the Obama administration works
feverishly to extend insurance coverage without upsetting established institutions, it is critical that we take stock of the full range
of reform possibilities, including roads not taken. This chapter first
examines the philosophical foundation behind the modern claims
of the right to health care before turning to the two major policy
initiatives that are now under consideration: the first is a single-
payer health-care system based on the Canadian model; the second,
more eclectic effort hopes to build on existing public and private
programs to extend basic coverage. I support neither of these
efforts. The simplest and most cogent objection is that they are too
costly, as no government can successfully devise rules to constrain

demand while seeking to drive to zero the health care costs of recipients. Accordingly, in the last section I present an alternative approach that stresses deregulation, which, by reining in health care, expands access to health-care services for those now excluded from the system.

A RIGHT TO HEALTH CARE

The Obama administration has begun with the premise articulated in the Democratic National Platform for 2008: "Every American man, woman, and child be guaranteed affordable, comprehensive health care." Such a program is a far cry from the now disfavored market-based system that gives all individuals the right, not to a claim against the state but to purchase whatever mix of goods and services they can from willing vendors. That market system does not impose any direct costs on the government and generates powerful pressures to reduce costs. But market solutions must meet serious problems of their own. Information about health care is hard to assemble and interpret. Huge payments for emergency treatments call for insurance companies, which have problems of their own in dealing with moral hazard and adverse selection issues. Insured people often exhibit riskier behavior than do those who are uninsured. People who are likely to become sick flock to insurance companies. But even in a competitive market, many people lack money to pay for basic treatment that everyone regards as appropriate. Unless supplemented by charitable contributions, voluntary markets could leave some people out in the cold.

Such objections explain the enormous political pressures to create positive rights to health care, understood here as direct claims against the government to either supply or fund health-care services. The hard question is whether that approach is more imperfect than the market alternatives that might be strengthened in its stead.

Unfortunately, the fixation on health care ignores a key insight: health outcomes depend not only on health care but also on all personal activities that enhance or detract from the quality of our lives. Give younger people high disposable incomes, and they will drive cars with better tires, eat better food, and live in nicer places, all of which reduce the likelihood that they will need medical care. Easing general taxation burdens saves the lives of people who now die before reaching the emergency room by allowing them to purchase on their own similar goods and services that prolong and make it possible to enjoy life while they are still healthy. For all the huge expenditures on Medicare, since its inception in 1965, life expectancy past the age of sixty-five has only gone up a few years. So beware of all those true stories of people who lack desperately needed medical care; such testimonials don't explain the background conditions that make their illnesses so acute.

By missing such broader themes, the Obama team is likely to champion counterproductive and costly measures that will put a health-care system already in distress on the critical list. At every step we must all remember that rights are easy to announce but difficult to fund. Because it is never clear in principle just who should pick up the tab, governments struggle to tap new sources of revenue, not to improve market institutions. The Obama administration, deaf to market arguments, worries exclusively about how best to implement the positive right to health care. The two major possibilities—single-payer and building on existing programs—both have serious pitfalls.

Single-Payer Systems

In 1993, the Clinton administration spearheaded an abortive campaign for a single-payer health-care system patterned on the Canadian model, which guarantees all its citizens affordable health care regardless of their ability to pay. Its commitment to centralized financing, however, does *not* mean that the government runs the system. Instead, the Canadian national government distributes funds to the provinces, which in turn enter into various service and fee arrangements with health-care providers. A strong budgetary thumb, however, has created extended queues for services, with some of the excess demand being supplied in the United States, and postponed investments in modern medical equipment. In recent years, the cost increases have paralleled those in the United States, albeit from a lower initial base. It is an open question as to whether to count the Canadian system as a success. Yet even if the Canadian system were flawless in design, it is doubtful that it could be transferred in its entirety into the very different political arrangements and cultural expectations in the United States. Our hodgepodge arrangements cannot be easily rationalized.

In evaluating the above prospects we should take heed of why the Clinton plan failed. That mammoth proposal was defeated, at least in part, because it left unclear whether ordinary individuals could purchase additional health-care insurance outside the nationalized plan. Such private options are allowed in England but have been fiercely resisted in Canada, where they are seen as the source and symbol of an unacceptable two-tier system of health-care entitlements. Such egalitarian sentiments in the United States were not—and are not—as intense. The uncertainties over extra coverage created a large backlash against the Clinton plan. Many Americans believe strongly in *minimum* health-care entitlements but oppose any system that imposes *maximum* health-care limits.

The doubters have a point. It is easy to attack the rich for spending their money on frivolities; it is also easy to attack them for spending their money on necessities. Together, the two prohibitions point to a system of perfect income equality, which, no matter how disguised, stifles initiative, hard work, and innovation. In the long run, that self-destructive constraint reduces the labor of our most productive citizens, which in turn erodes the wealth base needed for any redistributive program. Any Obama health-care plan will have to make peace with at least some inequalities; maximum limits on the private purchase of health care are out.

The second difficulty with an American single-payer system is that of scale. What might work for twenty-five million people in Canada is not likely to work for the more than three hundred million people in the United States. No one could figure out how to divide the nation into operational subdivisions in the Clinton years, and no one can do it today. For example, separating cities and suburbs into different units would have enormous ramifications for the cost and quality of care that people would receive under alternative configurations of the health-care system.

The third difficulty with any single-payer plan is captured in its name. Single-payer creates another state monopoly that carries with it the same baggage as all other monopolies. Price competition would come to a halt, as would innovations in new services; funding for basic research in health care could easily decline. Patients would be either restricted in or denied their choice of hospitals, physicians, and ancillary services. To be sure, any sensible single-payer plan would try to mitigate such problems, but how?

The root problem here is that a single-payer monopoly does not try to maximize its profits—at which point it would cut down on services. Instead, it tries to give away the services at as low a cost as possible. But it has no idea which mechanism to substitute for price in rationing services. King Canute could not stop the tides; a lumbering government agency cannot hold payments down for patients and prop wages up for hospitals, physicians, and other health-care providers. Medicare has never been able to achieve those dual goals, and a broader plan will face even greater pressures. Ideally, we would supply medical care to all individuals until the marginal cost of additional services exceeds their marginal benefits. But no one has any idea of how to implement such a regime. Supplying health care at zero or low cost stimulates demand even for those who must bear the costs and risks of treatment. Under conditions of scarcity, some people who need care must do without it, but who? The blunt truth is that administrative guidelines are made to be evaded; only a price system can cut back on demand, especially when some of the cases crying out for treatment come from people who cannot pay for it. So if the Obama administration chooses to abandon single-payer health care, what should it put in its place?

EXPAND FROM THE EXISTING BASE

Plan B calls for extending the reach of health care by building on public and private programs now in place, with the first prong of the strategy expanding eligibility to existing programs, as witnessed the rapid passage of SCHIP in the opening weeks of the Obama administration. In its initial incarnation SCHIP covered about seven million children not poor enough to participate in Medicaid but not fortunate enough to have private insurance. The program's expanded access will substantially benefit the children who receive the care, but its long-term consequences could undermine its short-term gains. Early evidence suggests that the number of employers now offering health insurance to children has dwindled from 69 to 60 percent, and we could easily see such a cycle repeated, with the expansion of SCHIP leading to a further contraction of the voluntary market, followed by additional expansions of eligibility in SCHIP.

Most SCHIP supporters prefer to think of the program as a down payment on universal health care. But at this point, the worries over a single-payer plan loom large. Its early detection programs may reduce the heavy costs of health care down the road, but its implicit heavy subsidies could also lead to a vast increase in the demand for less-essential services that become affordable only at subsidized prices. The unresolved long-term question is whether this program is sustainable in the long run, which Medicare is not, as evident in the grim annual reports prepared by Medicare trustees.

Similar observations apply to Medicare Part D, a new entitlement program introduced by the Bush administration in 2006 that deals with prescription drugs. Its subsidy for prescriptions is incorporated into a system that encourages health benefit plans to compete actively for customers, which has happily lowered the cost below the original projections. CMS (an imperfect acronym for the Center of Medicare & Medicaid Services) had originally estimated the costs of Medicare Part D at $634 billion, but estimates from 2008 dropped that figure to $395 billion. The Obama administration may seek to inject the United States into the market as a monopsony buyer of drugs to lower their costs further. Yet that approach appears to be doubly uninformed: it is always a mistake to tinker with any government program that works, and any effort to drive prices lower is likely to have a negative effect on research and development.

Unfortunately, this prospect is far from remote; drug companies are already reeling from a broad array of regulations and restrictions, including tough terms of sale in foreign markets dominated by local governments; increased expense and duration of clinical trials under stringent FDA rules; more uncertain patent protection, including protection against reimportation at low prices; expanded liability under state tort law; mandated sales to state Medicaid programs at low prices; the constant specter of general price controls; and increased restrictions on sales techniques in both the consumer and the physician market. No recent regulatory change in the pharmaceutical space has been of help to private firms that supply patented drugs. In this area, as in so many others, the risk of government overreach is real. The president may have lifted the legal restrictions on stem-cell research, but the landscape remains precarious for research in this area.

Private employer and insurance benefit programs. The Obama administration is also likely to build on the employer-based private health plans now in place for most Americans, with his mantra being that "if you like your current health plan, keep it." The point of this message is to underscore the differences between Clinton in 1993 and Obama in 2009. The Obama health-care plan does not impose uniform standards of health care on all individuals; nor does it force everyone to do business with a government monopolist. Instead it goes to great length to preserve choice to the extent feasible. In addition, it calls for offering a range of options to those who are unsatisfied with the current system, including coverage "similar to what members of Congress enjoy."

The coercive portion of the Obama health-care plan, however, lies in its treatment of those employers who do not currently supply health insurance to their employees. A new "pay or play" regime will require such firms to pay taxes into the public coffers or provide health insurance to their workers. The program also requires that health insurance be purchased at some minimum figure— $6,000 or upward for a family—that could not be offset by wage reductions for those workers who earn close to the minimum wage, with the likely result being increased unemployment. The pressure on insurance plans is further tightened by mandates prohibiting insurance companies from charging higher prices to those with pre-existing conditions.

In tandem, those multiple restrictions could easily gut the private building blocks on which the Obama program for national health care rests. Private health insurance is not a fixed fact of nature. Health plans regularly alter their cost and coverage in response to pressures on both supply and demand. Even if the federal government did not put its thumb on the scale, the shifts in law, population, and technology would continue to reconfigure those plans in the future as they have done in the past. New mandates, applied at the employer or the insurer level, could easily force insurers to contract or fold. An Obama requirement that restricts employers and insurers from discriminating against persons with preexisting conditions could further eviscerate employer-based insurance.

Traditional insurance in voluntary markets was not a form of "social insurance" intended to both pool risk and redistribute wealth from one person to another. Rather, traditional insurance companies set rates to bleed out cross-subsidies across the insured by matching premiums with anticipated risks. The gains to all players come from smoothing the risk over time, not from getting someone else to pay for their losses. Any requirement that firms not discriminate in accordance with perceived risk requires that healthy persons overpay on a prospective basis so that sick people can underpay. Healthy individuals will leave such plans, unless coerced to remain. The Democratic National Platform calls for firms to compete on service, "not on their ability to avoid or overcharge people who are or may get sick." But sound competition works on all margins. The ablest firm cannot survive if its operations cannot cover its anticipated losses. One response is for insurers to package their coverage to discourage high-risk patients whom they can only serve at a loss. But if such devices are forbidden, the ablest firms can be driven into bankruptcy precisely because they are attractive to the sickest patients. Yet it is unlikely that any federal action would, or could, design an assigned-risk pool (like those for high-risk drivers) that would help insurers avoid insolvency. Left unchecked, employers will drop health-care insurance as insurance companies flee the field.

The situation will only get worse as Congress and the states pile on new mandates. For example, the recent bailout legislation included the Paul Wellstone Mental Health and Addiction Equity Act of 2008, which requires that every element of coverage supplied for physical ailments be carried over to these illnesses, which private insurance carriers often exclude from coverage for good economic reasons. Addiction is in part a willful condition that could become more common precisely because insurance coverage for it is now available. Moreover, the high costs for a small fraction of the workforce will drive up rates for everyone else. Mental health hazards are difficult to detect and monitor, and the base rates for insurance must reflect those differences. Because these risks are more acute in some patient populations than in others, some employer plans may well perish owing to cost; other plans will adjust rates to make them less desirable than before. The illusion that any insurance coverage will remain constant when all else is in flux is a form of naiveté that will hasten the destruction of the voluntary market on the path to national health care.

The cost pressures of the Obama proposals have now hit home. In March 2009, Obama indicated that he might let (a Democratic) Congress back off from his State of the Union pledge not to alter the current tax rule that allows employers to deduct their premiums on employee health care from gross income without requiring the employees to take the fair market value of the plan into taxable income. This proposal will bleed much of the current subsidy out of health care, which is welcome as a matter of first principle. But the proposal also undercuts any effort to make current private health plans the linchpin of a new national health-care system. The added tax revenues will not be used to reduce overall tax rates but will help fund the costs of insuring uninsured or underinsured people. Ordinary taxpayers will experience declines in their disposable income that will in turn reduce their demand for health-care coverage. Without corrective action, the present system will unravel.

The pressures will only intensify if the Obama administration keeps its pledge to provide ordinary people with additional health-care options "similar to those that Members of Congress enjoy." That statement rests on a deep misunderstanding of insurance underwriting. It is always possible to offer the same *formal* coverage to ordinary people that Congress now provides for itself. But the composition of the two risk pools is so radically different that they cannot be funded at anything close to the same cost. It costs a lot more to service a random draw of the population than it does members of Congress under identical policies. Indeed, the economy will rapidly deteriorate if the sickest people are allowed to buy policies whose costs cannot be covered by existing revenue sources.

How then to fund these new ambitions? Largely by mirrors it seems. The Obama health plan seeks to cover the costs by bleeding key inefficiencies into the provision of health care. But it can't deliver. The Obama administration envisions "state-of-the-art health information technology systems, privacy-protected medical records, reimbursement incentives," and independent review boards to make sure the people get the right drugs at the right time. All this is said to yield an annual savings of $2,500 per family, which, with a 100 million families, clocks out at $250 billion per year. That huge number, if realized, still buys us only a two-year respite in health-care cost increases. But the savings are unlikely to materialize at all. Electronic records don't come cheap for single institutions, many of which have already foundered at the task. New technology requires expensive up-front costs, which are complicated by the need to transition away from older systems onto newer ones. State and private hospitals have already started off in different directions, hampering efforts at unification. The effort to bring millions of new individuals into a single integrated system, often with sketchy data, will be mammoth. The mundane business of data entry introduces errors into the records that are hard to undo, even if the system is continuously updated. Perhaps a program like this will pay for itself in a decade, but it can't offer a short-term fix for today's budget flows.

Similarly, the effort to improve reimbursement schemes has been a Medicare mantra since the early Reagan years. But each new government protocol is quickly neutralized when hospitals switch billing strategies in response to the government initiative. The costs of the Obama plan are real. Its savings are largely mythical. There is no balanced budget in this nation's future. There is only the relentless movement to a single-payer plan from which there will likely be an opt-out provision allowing some well-to-do individuals to get decent health care.

An Alternative Reform Proposal

This glum assessment of the Obama approach to health care begins with the premise that it is easier to enact entitlements than it is to pay for them. What is needed is a fresh approach that does not seek new sources of revenue to pay for unlimited access without compromising quality. Rather the appropriate line of attack addresses cost directly, using better control of costs to ease the pressure on access. The principle here is simple: lower costs will bring into the marketplace individuals who cannot afford health-care coverage under the current system. Unfortunately, the Obama approach does not mention one specific regulatory program *now in place* that it will repeal or slim down. Nor was one market-oriented individual or organization invited to participate in the Obama health-care summit held in March 2009 (see http://spectator.org/archives/2009/03/11/ostracized-by-obama/print). But many regulations cry out for reconsideration.

The first such step would turn its back on government mandates for private coverages such as the recent Wellstone Act. The philosophy behind mandates rests on the strong conviction that any denial of coverage for a particular condition signals a market failure that requires government intervention. The correct way to read all mandates, however, is as implicit taxes that undo considered market judgments that certain coverages cost more than they are worth. There is no reason to impose a mandate if a private employer or insurer already offers coverage. No insurance company has an incentive to turn down any line of business from which it can turn a profit. But it has every incentive to turn down a line of business that will cost consumers (and their informed intermediaries) more for coverage than they are willing to pay.

When government mandates certain coverages, it does more than create an administrative headache; it in effect imposes a loss on employees, employers, and insurers who have chosen not to include the specified coverage, dangers that go unnoticed when absorbed without a reduction in coverage. Thus, assume that for some workers the mandate costs $50 per month more than it is worth but that their implicit gain (often called consumer surplus) from the underlying insurance contract is $100 per month. Those workers will keep the policy and absorb the loss. But now reverse the numbers: suppose that the new mandate imposes a net loss of $100 per month for a policy that previously generated only a $50 per month surplus and that the coverage will be dropped, adding to the ranks of the uninsured. The combined impact of multiple mandates only exacerbates the overall situation. In short, we can have extensive coverage for a few people or modest coverage for many. We cannot have extensive coverage for many individuals. Strong mandates increase the ranks of the uninsured.

The issue of mandates is only one instance whereby a disregard of sound contracting principles imposes taxes that reduce overall coverage. The simmering malpractice crisis is best understood as a judicial mandate for extensive tort damages that costs consumers more than it is worth, resulting in higher insurance premiums and withdrawal of medical services when costs become prohibitive. Unfortunately, the Obama approach refuses to treat high malpractice premiums as a sign of distress. Rather, it regards them as an open invitation for price controls on medical malpractice insurers that will drive them from the market, thereby exacerbating the underlying problem of health-care delivery.

The list goes on. One of the most intrusive and costly systems of health regulation is HIPAA, or the Health Insurance Portability and Accountability Act, which President Clinton signed into law in 1996 and which has been a chronic administrative headache ever since. Before HIPAA, the reported instances of troublesome invasions of privacy and misuse of data, especially in psychiatric cases, were negligible. Those cases that did occur were met with stern administrative or judicial sanctions. HIPAA was meant to be primarily directed at the transference of insurance coverage between jobs, which turned out to be a less serious problem than expected. But its baroque privacy regulations create endless nightmares on the ground and will vastly complicate any effort to set up a comprehensive electronic network. Repealing this bill would most likely save significantly more than the $25 billion that the total system would cost.

Another promising area for reform is state restrictions on licensing for both out-of-state physicians and insurance companies. Let us assume that licensing is necessary to preserve a minimum level of medical and health-care services. In that case, adopt a simple rule saying that anyone who has practiced for five years in his or her home state has a license to practice anywhere, without undergoing a third-degree investigation with anticompetitive motives. More important, allow the free entry of businesses into the health-care market, including Wal-Mart, Target, or any new player. Why use emergency rooms as the provider of last resort? Well-run private systems can pick up the slack at a fraction of the cost, in part by substituting sophisticated systems and protocols for individual physician judgments, which are often unreliable in practice. The same approach should work for hospital care, where competition is now hobbled by the need for certificates of need. Open up entry and local monopolies will lose their dominance. Similarly a relaxation on the sale of insurance across state lines would increase competition. Note that all these proposals loosen regulatory chains: none of them require new budget appropriation, and all open up new sources of taxable revenues. Ultimately their combined effect should reduce the pressures on government funding of health care. Lower costs would then increase the private utilization of health care.

CONCLUSION

Reforming health care will not take place if all government does is tweak current political solutions. Instead, it is imperative to ransack the statute books, state and federal, to weed out all the counterproductive regimes that stifle competition and raise cost. Unless this is done, the drift toward a single-payer system will be inexorable, for the defects of bad regulation will be treated as conclusive evidence of the inherent defects of unregulated markets. Yet the proper approach can slow down, and perhaps stop, the endless cycle of government taxes and transfer payments to facilitate broader access and higher levels of affordable care. Obama's bromides will not cut the Gordian knot.

8 A Mad Scramble for Infrastructure Dollars

James L. Huffman

In response to then president-elect Obama's proposal for a massive stimulus plan to include large sums for infrastructure construction and repair, America 2050, a panel of twenty-six of the nation's infrastructure experts, issued a statement of principles for effective infrastructure spending. "When it comes to infrastructure, America has been flying blind," said the panel. "We should invest in projects that achieve job creation in the short run while creating the foundation for long-term economic success and energy independence."

Early indications are that the Obama administration continues to fly blind, despite assurances to the contrary. Although it speaks of a disciplined effort to ensure that infrastructure funding is not wasted but used only on job-stimulating and economic growth-promoting projects, the mad flurry of activity in the first hundred days has led to a rush for the money, with no rational system for ensuring that the stated goals are achieved.

Driven by a desire to achieve instant economic results, the administration has created intense competition within and between states for infrastructure funding. The pot of money is large—about fifty billion dollars—but when spread across the nation it gets thinner. The American Association of State Highway and Transportation Officials announced that it could spend all the fifty billion, plus fourteen billion more, on five thousand "ready-to-go" highway and bridge projects. The nation's mayors offered a list of 11,391 infrastructure projects in 427 cities requiring seventy-three billion. Transit officials have 736 shovel-ready projects costing over twelve billion. Absent a well-conceived system for allocating these funds, political rent seeking, not good infrastructure policy, will be the result.

The chapter examines the rationale behind my principal conclusions, which follow:

1. Despite the unprecedented commitment of federal taxpayer dollars in the American Recovery and Reinvestment Act of 2009 (ARRA), the 2009 Omnibus Appropriations Act, and President Obama's proposed 2010 budget, the nation's infrastructure will remain dramatically underfunded as long as we continue to rely exclusively on federal taxpayer funding. Obama administration policies do little to facilitate or encourage the private investment necessary to meet the nation's infrastructure challenges.

2. Although the president has issued guidelines to ensure that ARRA funding achieves programmatic results, provides economic stimulus, and achieves long-term public benefits, the existing bureaucratic structure, combined with the persistence of legislative earmarks and the realities of congressional politics, guarantee that federal infrastructure funding will continue to be largely ad hoc.

3. Favoring public over private supply of infrastructure and a barely visible commitment to market assessments of supply and demand make it almost impossible for the federal government to prioritize infrastructure investments in relation to both other competing infrastructure projects and other categories of federal spending.

4. The long-term economic growth benefits of enacted and proposed infrastructure spending will be far less than those
   claimed by the Obama administration because of its inability
   to prioritize economically and its conflicting policy objectives.

President Obama's
Infrastructure Initiatives

During the campaign, candidate Obama made frequent reference to
the need for investment in both maintenance and repair of existing
infrastructure and the creation of new twenty-first-century infrastructure adapted to a digital and green future. With respect to both
objectives, candidate Obama had widespread support. The American Society of Civil Engineers estimates that it would take $2.2 tril-
lion from all levels of government to bring America's roads,
bridges, and water-related infrastructure into a state of good repair.
Other estimates of the nation's infrastructure deficit range from
$1.6 to $3.5 trillion. With respect to new infrastructure, there is
wide-ranging agreement on a need for constant improvement,
along with widely varying cost estimates. Just for a "smart grid"
that would increase efficiencies in electricity use and distribution,
estimates range from $100 to $400 billion during the next decade.

Anticipations were that as much as half or more of the stimulus
package would go for infrastructure. The reality is very different.
Less that 13 percent of the funds appropriated in the American
Recovery and Reinvestment Act of 2009 (ARRA) is dedicated to
infrastructure, even broadly defined. A more realistic accounting
puts the infrastructure share at about 7 percent. President Obama
has also signed the Omnibus Appropriations Act of 2009, which
does nothing to change infrastructure spending priorities. Indeed
much of the infrastructure spending in that bill is in the form of
thousands of "earmarks," a special-interest budgeting tactic the
new president had promised to end.

President Obama's proposed 2010 budget includes a less than 3 percent increase over 2009 and 2008 infrastructure spending, an amount that will barely dent the existing maintenance deficit, leaving little for new infrastructure development. The president is proposing a five-year, five-billion-dollar state grant program for high-speed rail, but that, too, barely dents the forty billion estimated cost of high-speed rail in California alone. The proposed 2010 Department of Energy budget includes an unspecified amount for the smart grid, but overall the department's 2010 budget is unchanged from the projected 2009 budget, all of which is before the earmarkers in Congress get their hands on the budget.

The modest projected infrastructure spending in the 2010 budget is not surprising, given the massive increase in federal debt accumulated in just the opening three months of the Obama administration. For the same reason, there is little chance we will see significant increases in infrastructure funding in the next few budget cycles. Although we will see modest investments in digital and "green" projects, these are likely to be largely symbolic. Absent dramatic increases in funding, the biggest infrastructure issues for President Obama are how to prioritize and manage the expenditure of existing resources.

The president's total surrender on earmarks in the omnibus spending bill does not bode well for a new and better approach. On March 20, however, the president did issue directives on the expenditure of ARRA funds that focus on transparency and limiting the influence of registered lobbyists but do little to jump-start a system for prioritizing federal infrastructure spending. The president does call for "merit-based selection criteria" meant to assure that ARRA funding (1) achieves programmatic results, (2) provides economic stimulus, and (3) achieves long-term public benefits. But those criteria are to be applied by department and agency heads who remain free to define programs and operate independently. Absent fundamental change to the existing federal structure for funding, construction, and maintenance of infrastructure, the president's directives will have little effect; future appropriations bills will continue to be loaded with funding for local projects having no necessary relation to national infrastructure priorities.

After talk of three or four hundred billion for infrastructure, ARRA was a disappointment for infrastructure proponents. However the thousands of items in the 407-page bill are categorized, the total falls far short of projected needs. Using the broadest possible definition of infrastructure, ARRA contains approximately $100 billion of authorized spending. If all these funds were applied to reducing the existing infrastructure deficit (based on the most conservative estimate of $1.6 trillion), it would take sixteen years of annual appropriations at the same level to accomplish the task. But less than half of the $100 billion is destined for infrastructure of the type included in the deficit estimates, and a significant share of that will go for new facilities rather than maintaining existing infrastructure. In addition, the administration's emphasis on shovel-ready projects means that much of the funding will go for projects that were already funded, allowing state and local governments to divert those funds to deficit reduction or other uses.

In summary, ARRA includes thirty billion dollars for highways and bridges, including those on Indian and federal lands; nearly seven billion for transit; six billion for clean water; four billion for the Army Corps of Engineers; two and a half billion for airports, including one billion to the Transportation Security Administration for explosives-detection machines; more than one billion for rural utilities; and one billion for military facilities. The development of high-speed rail gets eight billion, a fraction of the anticipated costs for a national system, and the much-ballyhooed smart grid gets four and a half billion, less than 5 percent of the most optimistic estimates of the cost.

But if it falls far short of actual infrastructure needs, ARRA does include something for just about everyone under the infrastructure heading. There is fifty million dollars apiece for the Central Utah

Project and the California Bay Delta; $375 million for Corps of Engineers projects on the Mississippi River, a billion each for veterans' hospitals, community development, and the Bureau of Reclamation; twenty-five million for the Smithsonian; seven hundred million for the National Park Service; $140 million for the Coast Guard; one and a half billion for homelessness prevention and rehousing; two billion for redevelopment of abandoned and foreclosed homes; three hundred million for diesel emission reduction; fifty million for the preservation and restoration of national cemeteries and monuments; fifteen million for the preservation of historically black colleges and universities; and much, much more.

The enacted 2009 Omnibus Act contains even more of a grab bag of spending. Many of the nine thousand earmarks in the act are for infrastructure but with no pretence that these projects are part of a program of prioritized spending. The same is sure to be true of the 2010 spending bill, unless President Obama finds the political will to eliminate earmarks. On that campaign promise he has failed once and is likely to fail again. Despite Senator William Proxmire's Golden Fleece Awards of the 1970s and 1980s, outrage in the 2008 presidential election over Alaska's "bridge to nowhere" and candidate Obama's pledge to eliminate them, earmarks have increased from ten in 1982 to five hundred in 1991, six thousand in 2005, and nine thousand in 2009.

Although President Obama's proposed 2010 budget does contain funding for high-speed rail, the smart grid, and other infrastructure innovations, the amounts proposed are a fraction of what the systems are projected to cost. An even bigger problem is that they conform to the modal approach of earlier federal budgets. Those budgets funded infrastructure on the basis of various modes of transportation and other public goods and services, with separate budgets for highways, public transit, airports and air travel, ports and water navigation, and so on and now budgets for the smart grid, for health information services, and for green infrastructure.

That modal approach, combined with the rigid structure of the federal bureaucracy, ensure that integrated infrastructure planning and prioritization is impossible.

Finally, President Obama has embraced the concept of a National Infrastructure Reinvestment Bank, first suggested in 2007 by the Commission on Public Infrastructure at the Center for Strategic and International Studies. According to the president, "repairs will be determined not by politics, but by what will maximize our safety and homeland security; what will keep our environment clean and economy strong." In the commission's vision, the bank would exist not to overcome inefficiencies in capital markets but rather to bring greater efficiency to the expenditure of federal funds and, critically, to raise additional funds from existing capital markets. In addition to drawing on private capital, the bank would circumvent the inefficient modal funding method. In the president's vision, the bank would invest $60 billion over ten years, far short of what is needed, but at least the concept holds the promise of overcoming some of the existing failings of federal infrastructure investment.

THE ROLE FOR FEDERAL
INFRASTRUCTURE SPENDING

Obvious examples of infrastructure are roads, bridges, sidewalks, sewer and water systems, railroads, telephone systems, air and water navigation systems, and the Internet. Building on property scholar Carol Rose's "comedy of the commons," some economists now count as infrastructure such natural systems as wetlands (providing water purification services), forests (carbon sequestration), air and water (pollution sinks), and bees (pollination). President Obama's March 20, 2009, directive on stimulus spending includes environmental protection as infrastructure.

Three characteristics define these and other resources as infrastructure: (1) the resource is in demand as an input to the production of other goods and services, (2) the resource can be consumed by a significant number of people without affecting the benefits experienced by other consumers, and (3) the resource is an input to a wide range of private, public, and nonmarket goods and services. Based on this definition, some of what the Obama administration has counted as infrastructure spending—weatherization of homes and homelessness prevention and rehousing, for example—is actually wealth transfers. Those transfers may create some new jobs in the weatherization and housing sectors but will necessarily take resources from other productive sectors of the economy.

The federal government's role in infrastructure spending should depend on the answers to three questions: (1) When should infrastructure be publicly supplied? (2) For publicly provided infrastructure, what type, quantity, and quality should be supplied? (3) Which public infrastructure should be supplied by the federal government, and which by state or local governments?

A mistaken presumption favoring public infrastructure. Beyond the pervasive call for more regulation and a renewed skepticism about markets, the administration has not evidenced overt opposition to private infrastructure. But there has been no suggestion from President Obama, his transportation secretary, or other administration officials that private ownership or participation might be preferable in some circumstances. Rather, in the rush to fund infrastructure projects to stimulate the economy, it is presumed that all the money, at least for traditional infrastructure such as roads and transit, will be spent directly by the government.

There is a risk that the current economic recession, which many blame on capitalist excess, will lead to skepticism about the experiments in private infrastructure that have occurred over the last two decades. Encouraged by several free market think tanks and some academic literature, state and local governments have privatized both ownership and management of infrastructure, including municipal water and sewer systems, highways, bridges, and solid waste collection and disposal. Those experiments have created opportunities for the investment of private capital in public infrastructure, and have generally worked well in terms of both quality of service and efficiency, although voters have sometimes objected, not surprisingly, when user fees are imposed for what were previously perceived to be free public services.

Several state, local, and foreign governments are far ahead of the federal government in encouraging private supply and management of infrastructure, relying on user fees and other market forces to better link infrastructure supply to demand, and reforming existing law to allow for public-private partnerships. The City of Oakland, California, for example, has recently reached an agreement for a private investment of $150 million in port facilities with promises of another $350 million. The State of Virginia is reviewing a $3.5-billion proposal from an Illinois company to take over management of the state's ports. Texas enacted legislation in 2003 (strengthened in 2005) to facilitate collecting highway tolls by means of public-private partnerships. California has recently adopted legislation enabling several such public-private partnerships. Pennsylvania governor Ed Rendell has proposed that his state lease the Pennsylvania Turnpike to a private operator to cope with a $1.7 billion annual shortfall in the commonwealth's budget for surface transportation infrastructure. Public-private highways, tunnels, and bridges are operating successfully in several other countries including Australia, Canada, France, and Italy.

To his credit, President Obama's 2010 transportation budget proposal does call for "better targeted spending to help communities explore innovative solutions like road pricing to reduce congestion." But there is no indication that the administration has considered public-private approaches like those noted above. Nor does it appear that the administration has heeded the February 2009 report of the National Surface Transportation Infrastructure

Financing Commission, which urges private-sector financial participation and user fee-based funding approaches. That report also
confirms that ARRA funding will have little impact on the short-
or long-range infrastructure funding challenges faced by the federal
government.

Rather than presume government should supply all infrastructure, the Obama administration should take the opportunity of the
interest in infrastructure to develop good policies on its public and
private provision. The National Research Council provides guidance to developing such policies: "Infrastructure is a means to other
ends, and the effectiveness, efficiency, and reliability of its contribution to these other ends must ultimately be the measure of infrastructure performance."

Bridges to nowhere and many other projects funded by congressional earmarks, including projects funded under ARRA and the
2009 Omnibus Spending Bill, whether public or private, will fail
that performance test. But many projects that meet the test will pass
with even higher marks if privately owned or managed. The key is
in knowing which projects should be public and which private.
Nothing in the Obama policy pronouncements suggests criteria for
making that decision: no suggestion that federal infrastructure
funding might be better spent by subsidizing or financing private
providers or any encouragement for state and local governments to
explore that option. Generally, the presumption is that all the funds
will be invested in publicly provided infrastructure.

The public provision of infrastructure is generally justified on
the basis that the infrastructure in question is a public good or that
it provides significant external benefits; both of these justifications,
however, amount to the same thing. A public good is one from
which consumers cannot be readily excluded and which can be
consumed by many without affecting the benefits to others, making
the benefits from which consumers cannot be excluded, by definition, external. So whether described as public goods or external

benefits, the obstacle to private provision is that the supplier cannot readily collect a fee from consumers.

When the infrastructure in question is a public good, there can be no competitive market for it, meaning that the efficiency benefits of a market are absent. Through competitive bidding for the opportunity to supply the public good, however, efficiency gains can be realized in precisely the same way that the government benefits from competitive bidding among private contractors for constructing roads and bridges. Although competitive bidding can be, and sometimes is, corrupted by political influence, that failure in implementation does not diminish the benefits that can flow from true competition among private suppliers of public goods.

Although highways are often pointed to as an example of a public good to be publicly provided, they actually illustrate that the matter is not so simple. In the case of local streets and roads, the near impossibility of excluding nonpayers makes government provision the only option. But, as some states learned with the toll road precursors to the interstate highway system, it is possible to exclude nonpayers from a limited-access highway. Even though this did not, at the time, lead to private ownership or operation of segments of the interstate highway system, it did introduce direct user fees into the provision of highways. Today, even for local streets and roads, the public goods presumption is no longer valid, given the technology that allows for the congestion pricing of road use.

Even when technology has not solved the exclusion problem sufficiently to create a private market, other external benefits (public goods) may result from infrastructure. In that case a private supplier will undersupply the good or service because the demand is limited to those who pay for its benefits. For example, railroads and airlines function as private enterprises with sufficient revenues from freight and passengers to cover their costs. But many benefits to nonpassengers and nonshippers derive from efficient transportation systems. Because these beneficiaries pay nothing to the railroad or airline, an undersupply of both services will ensue unless public subsidies provide an optimum level of those external benefits.

Such external benefits sometimes lead to the same presumption that favors the public provision of infrastructure. The central insight of Carol Rose's work on the commons is that various non-market public benefits derive from open access to resources. Because open access implies public ownership, it is easy to conclude that infrastructure resources providing significant external benefits should be supplied free of charge by the government. But the comedy of the commons does not repeal the tragedy of the commons. Although open access to publicly provided infrastructure may yield significant social benefits, it can also deplete those resources when one person's use affects the amount or quality of supply available to others. Even when the marginal cost from additional consumers is zero, the public supplier does not escape the need to determine how much to supply. Both over- and undersupply of infrastructure negatively affect net social welfare.

How much to spend on what? Whether infrastructure is supplied publicly or privately, a second question is the kind, amount, and quality to supply. A clear advantage of privately owned and maintained infrastructure is the supplier's ability to resolve both those issues on the basis of market demand. The existence of external benefits might justify a government subsidy or providing a larger supply, but, absent a method of measuring the forgone external benefits, there is no way to ensure that subsidized infrastructure is not oversupplied. Because all infrastructure comes at a cost, the opportunity costs of oversupply may be as much or more than the forgone benefits of undersupply.

True to past practice, the Obama administration is taking a supply-side approach to determine how much to spend on what, with the assumption that use will grow with expanding supply. Little attention is paid to demand, largely because, absent a market, the only indicators of demand are congestion and political pressure.

Congestion may be an indication of insufficient supply but not necessarily because consumers of most public infrastructure are paying only indirectly (through taxes) if at all. Under those circumstances the apparent demand will be higher than it would be in a market where consumers pay the full market price; thus the amount supplied is likely to be greater than optimal.

As between different types of infrastructure there has been little in the way of systematic prioritization. Roads, dams, drinking water systems, flood control levees, environmental protection, or other types of infrastructure have risen to the top at different times but generally in response to perceived crises or political winds. A cost/benefit analysis often has been used to assess whether particular projects can be justified, but little economic sophistication has been applied to choose among the various types of infrastructure in which government might invest its limited resources. That the levees of New Orleans went unrepaired for decades while the federal government invested in all manner of local projects to satisfy members of Congress is convincing evidence of the problem.

Such supply challenges argue for greater reliance on private infrastructure and user fees, which provide a measure of demand, reduce congestion, and can influence the behavior of users when the government has other policy objectives, including accounting for the external costs and benefits associated with infrastructure. For example, roads impose an array of environmental costs that are generally unaccounted for, no matter whether drivers have free access or pay a toll. Some city planners have argued for limiting the supply of roads to create congestion, thus encouraging drivers to find other less environmentally harmful modes of travel. User fees, however, based on the actual cost of providing the road plus an estimate of the environmental costs, can reduce congestion and account for those external costs. But there are also external benefits in the form of increased economic activity, precisely the benefits that lead to our thinking of roads as infrastructure. Without taking into account the demand for those external benefits, we will under-estimate demand and provide a less than optimal number of roads.

Other types of infrastructure are subject to similar supply and demand analyses. But they are complicated to get right, and there is no indication that the Obama infrastructure initiatives have made any effort to address such issues. As in determining the relative roles of the public and private sectors, it will require a major over-haul of the federal government's approach to funding, building, and maintaining infrastructure. Those changes will not come easily, but they must be made if we are to avoid wasting vast sums on unproductive and unneeded projects.

When should the Feds do it? Using the interstate highway system as a model, the tendency is to think that the federal government should provide all public infrastructure. Although that was cer-tainly the right approach to an integrated interstate highway sys-tem, it is clearly not the best approach to every case. When public benefits and costs are local and likely to vary from one community to the next, state and local governments are far better situated than the federal government to assess questions of supply and demand. In infrastructure planning and provision, as in many other areas of government activity, the principle of subsidiarity should determine which level of government is best. Public infrastructure should be provided at the least centralized level appropriate. A logical corol-lary of the subsidiarity principle is a presumption in favor of private infrastructure whenever the necessary markets exist or can be cre-ated. Markets are, after all, the least centralized method for allocat-ing scarce resources.

Although it is not apparent that the Obama administration has thought in those terms, the method of distributing ARRA funds will inadvertently give the subsidiarity principle some play, for, with few exceptions, ARRA infrastructure funds are being distributed on a per capita basis. Although states are competing for some funds, each state has a reasonable expectation of funding roughly proportionate to its population. This does not ensure that the funds will be well spent, but it does leave open the possibility that individual states will allocate infrastructure spending on the basis of priorities reflecting real demand and on some chance of promoting economic growth.

INFRASTRUCTURE SPENDING AS STIMULUS

A separate, but not independent, question is whether President Obama's infrastructure initiatives will stimulate the economy in the short run and promote economic growth in the long run. Estimates of the effect of infrastructure spending on job creation vary widely. The Obama administration has suggested that as many as 47,000 jobs can result from investment of one billion dollars. A study done for the Alliance of American Manufacturers (AAM) puts the number at 18,000 jobs per billion invested. California governor Schwarzenegger recently announced that 11,000 jobs would result from an investment of $625 million in infrastructure, a ratio similar to the lower estimate of the AAM.

Estimates of second-order impacts (the external benefits that define particular goods as infrastructure) also vary widely. The work of David Aschauer in the late 1980s for the Federal Reserve Bank of Chicago, which is widely relied on, forecasts dramatic returns on public investment in infrastructure. But other studies indicate that in every decade since 1950, returns on public investment have been between a quarter to a half of those on private investment and that public investment in infrastructure can even have negative economic effects. The difficulty in forecasting growth benefits from public infrastructure investment derives from the absence of reliable measures of demand, particularly where infrastructure is supplied free of charge. Public infrastructure investment can have negative impacts on growth because, absent reliable demand estimates, infrastructure can be oversupplied, thus diverting resources from more productive investments.

On behalf of the Obama administration, Christina Romer and Jared Bernstein projected 3.7 percent GDP growth and 3,675,000 new jobs as a result of the ARRA stimulus package. Nobel laureate economist Gary Becker expressed skepticism on two grounds: "The activities stimulated by the package to a large extent would draw labor and capital away from other productive activities. In addition, the government programs were unlikely to be as well planned as the displaced private uses of these resources."

The first point is supported by an analysis by Forbes publications showing that most of the jobs created under ARRA will be for specialists with currently low rates of unemployment. The second point is underscored by the pressures to spend the infrastructure funding quickly in a circumstance of intense political competition; politics, not planning, is almost certain to prevail. Becker also reminds us that sooner or later these expenditures must be paid for by increased taxes. Anticipating those taxes will counter much of whatever stimulus effect the short-term spending might provide.

Potential stimulus benefits of infrastructure spending are also undercut by competing objectives. Emphasis on green infrastructure, combined with existing regulatory constraints, means that costs per unit will be higher and benefit per dollar spent will be lower. Similar effects are existing labor regulations such as the Davis-Bacon Act, which mandates prevailing wages on public works projects, and ARRA's Buy America requirement, which requires U.S. production of all iron, steel, and manufactured goods used in public buildings and public works.

CONCLUSION

Although the Obama administration has clearly underestimated the magnitude of the nation's infrastructure deficit and overestimated its capacity to rationalize the allocation of federal investments in infrastructure, its general policy statements evidence an appreciation for the need to overcome the history of pork barrel funding of the nation's roads, bridges, water systems, and other basic infrastructure. Aside from the large shortfall in funding just for maintaining existing public infrastructure, a failing unlikely to be remedied given the president's other spending ambitions, the biggest failing of the Obama administration's infrastructure policies is its presumption that private suppliers and market forces have only bit parts to play. The most viable solution to the funding challenge is private capital. The best way to assure that public and private capital is wisely invested is greater reliance on the efficiencies inherent in the market.

9 Defending an Open World Economy

Jagdish Bhagwati

The London Summit's official communiqué on April 2 began by applauding an open economy and briefly, therefore, generalizing the celebration of free trade to openness in a broader sense, as strongly urged in my writings of early 2009. According to the official communiqué, "We believe that the only sure foundation for sustainable globalization and rising prosperity for all is an open world economy."

But, except for some attention to actions on the trade front in the "London Summit Outcomes" released in London, the communiqué did not follow through with any details on the many dimensions of the threat to openness, which include immigration and labor markets and direct foreign investment. We face those threats today, even as the twin crises on Wall Street and Main Street continue to afflict us. Neither can we find an impassioned and substantial case being made for openness, nor the necessity of defending it, by the prominent leaders of the G20.

In particular, where was President Obama, whose rhetorical powers are remarkable enough for him to have given yet another

---

Although I am broadly supportive of the stimulus package, the threats to openness are built directly into it, as with the Buy America provision that has already initiated a trade war with Canada, which has lost American markets and has retaliated against the provision. President Obama does not have the luxury of waiting to confront threats to openness until he fixes the economy; the two policies are intertwined.

of his famous speeches, this time on the virtues of free trade and openness and the perils of protectionism and mutually harmful xenophobia in our and others' policy making?

On the dangers to openness, let me begin with trade, go on to foreign investment, and then to immigration, touching the principal danger points that should have prompted and informed such a presidential speech. But first consider briefly the issue of why openness is worth defending.

Openness and the Postwar Experience

The post-World War II decades began with a divide between rich and poor countries. Rich countries sought to restore openness to the world economy through liberal reforms promoting trade, direct foreign investment, and immigration (recall the *gastarbeiter* programs that made European recovery possible). Poor countries, on the other hand, generally shied away from such policies, afraid that openness would have a malign impact.

But by the 1980s it was clear that the anti-openness model had brought grief to the poor countries. As the proponents of that discredited economic philosophy (often married to "antimarket fundamentalism") tried to sabotage the pro-openness reforms, proposing that we resurrect the prehistoric dinosaurs like Steven Spielberg, the answer to them was best provided in John Kenneth Galbraith's witticism about an opponent: "his tragedy is that his prescriptions have been tried."

So with rich and poor countries finally in sync about the advantages of openness on the three critical dimensions of trade, direct investment, and immigration, both shared in the unparalleled prosperity that those policies produced.

But the opponents of this openness had a new card up their sleeve. Prosperity gained, yes, they said, but the poor had lost. But now, after hearing passion on one side and patient facts on the other, there is virtual unanimity that the prosperity produced by pro-openness policies, in tandem with other reforms, helped lift nearly half a billion poor above the poverty line in less than two decades.

Even in the rich countries, the stagnation of workers' wages has had little to do with trade and the outward flow of direct investment or the inward flow of unskilled workers. My own empirical work, updated in 2004 in my book, *In Defense of Globalization* (Oxford, 2004), and the recent work of Robert Lawrence of The Kennedy School at Harvard argue that trade with the poor countries is likely to have moderated the pressure on wages from other causes, such as acute labor-saving technical changes. The work of Giovanni Peri of the University of California argues that for unskilled immigration as well.

The pro-openness economists therefore have nothing to apologize for: openness serves the cause of the poor in the poor countries and is likely to be working for unskilled workers in the rich countries. Thus the assault on openness that has arisen worldwide threatens those gains and must be stoutly opposed.

DANGERS TO OPENNESS TODAY

Let us consider the protectionism afflicting post-crisis trade, direct investment, and hiring and firing of immigrants, in turn.

A. Trade. Let me address three important ways in which the threat of protection in trade has arisen recently: Buy America provisions in the stimulus bill, the auto bailout, and the Obama embrace of labor standards in trade treaties (which is a form of insidious protectionism, as I explain below).

1. Buy America. The Buy America provision, inconsistent as it was with our World Trade Organization (WTO) obligations in the original House and Senate versions, has now been qualified by a new clause requiring that its application be consistent with the international obligations undertaken by the United States. Nonetheless, some protectionist defenses and aspects of it need to be addressed.

First, my brilliant Massachusetts Institute of Technology student Paul Krugman has argued that increased U.S. spending, as required today, would leak into demand for foreign goods, raising its cost to the United States in shape of increased debt. So there is a case for using protection to keep its impact on the United States itself: the Buy America provision would prompt others to imitate us; they would spend more and use protection to keep *their* increased spending to themselves. The result would be more spending (i.e., stimulus) worldwide and admittedly more such protection. But the cost of protection is small in any event, Krugman argues, especially compared to the benefits of increased spending that it would allegedly facilitate.

Unfortunately, we must reject the Krugman argument because its premises are implausible and violate what we have already observed. Plenty of evidence exists that others will retaliate and that, too, not in a fine-tuned fashion. As the post-Smoot-Hawley experience showed, trade wars are fought, not by the gentlemanly rules of English cricket but by the no-holds-barred rules of American freestyle wrestling. The cost of protection, which even at the best of times is estimated by the best economists on the subject (such as Robert Feenstra, who leads the National Bureau of Economic Research's Program on International Economics, and Paul Romer, whose work on growth is most highly regarded) to be on the high side, is likely to be even higher if we foolishly leave ourselves open to such trade wars.

Second, some spokespeople for the American Federation of Labor and Congress of Industrial Organizations (AFL-CIO) claim that the European Union denies us access to its government procurement in several sectors and thus we are entitled to retaliate, suspending its access to our procurement. But this is a misunderstanding of the nature of the 1995 Government Procurement Agreement (GPA) at the WTO. The signatories to it (forty nations in all) have listed their sectoral and other exclusions and inclusions; these do not match, of course, because the overall balance of "concessions" when the Uruguay Round was concluded and the WTO was launched extended across many sectors such as manufactures and rules such as antidumping. We cannot unilaterally suspend the obligations we undertook under the GPA as part of that overall balance. If we were to unilaterally violate our treaty obligations under President Obama, who has promised we will return to the rule of law and work with other nations rather than wielding a machete over their heads and aiming an AK-47 at their hearts to get our way, we would be no better than Libya or the first George W. Bush administration.

Finally, does the qualifier, inserted at Obama's insistence in the conference version that will now be law—that we will practice Buy America in a WTO-consistent way—protect us from the prospect of a trade war? Not likely. There are two problems.

This first would mean that we would now begin to exclude China, India, Brazil, and other nonsignatories to the GPA (the developing countries were *not* expected to sign the GPA, one may recall), with the result being that they, in turn, could retaliate against our exports in several WTO-consistent ways (e.g., through raising lower-applied tariffs toward the higher-bound tariffs, switching purchases of nuclear plants from General Electric to France and aircraft from Boeing to Airbus). Thus we would have a WTO-consistent trade war breaking out. President Obama has listened to critics, such as myself, in a January op-ed. in the *Financial Times,* and insisted on WTO-consistency; he now needs to step up to the plate and denounce raising trade barriers and discriminatory policies even when they are technically WTO-consistent.

The second is, as anyone who understands trade litigation already knows, inserting a qualifier on WTO consistency and leaving in the Buy America provisions means that any well-heeled lobby can persuade the relevant agencies to give it a Buy America exclusion (even of signatories to the GPA) by claiming that the exclusion was WTO-consistent. The lobby would expect to get away with such behavior unless the matter is brought before the WTO Dispute Settlement Mechanism by the adversely affected signatories. (Essentially, this is what happened with the Safeguards action against foreign steel soon after President George W. Bush first took office: the administration claimed that its action was WTO-consistent, although many claimed it was not; it was then declared to be inconsistent at the WTO.)

Whether or not they take us to the dispute settlement court at the WTO, the excluded signatories will likely retaliate. It seems more sensible therefore to eliminate the Buy America provision altogether, as Senator McCain properly suggested.

2. Bailouts. Because bailouts embody actual (versus implicit) subsidies, they are regulated by the 1995 Subsidies and Countervailing Mechanism (SCM). Any sectoral subsidies under the SCM agreement are considered "actionable" (with only two subsidies, for local content or exports, declared illegal). There is little doubt therefore that an auto bailout, which is limited to one sector, would be actionable under the SCM agreement; when confined only to Detroit and not extended to foreign transplants, the bailout raises further red flags.

In fact, as French president Sarkozy plans to help Peugeot and other French car firms through similar bailouts, the Obama and Sarkozy administrations need to sit down and see whether they can confine their assistance to the car industry to either restructuring under Chapter 11-style bankruptcy procedures or WTO-consistent nondiscriminatory consumer subsidy schemes that subsidize car purchases regardless of who has produced the cars. The bankruptcy procedures would be allowed as long as explicit subsidies are not included in the bankruptcy-defined restructuring (in any event, even with no SCM agreement on airline services, many airlines in the United States have resorted to Chapter 11 and survived; one,

Continental, has resorted to Chapter 11 twice and is now known as the Chapter 22 airline).

All this holds, of course, regardless of the *economic* wisdom of granting sectoral support to one industry when several are in recession, an issue on which there is much division in the country.

3. Labor and Environmental Standards. The preoccupation with labor and (domestic) environmental pollution standards in trade treaties and institutions is a form of "export protectionism," prompted largely by the unions' fear that trade with the poor countries is driving down U.S. workers' wages. If you believe that, and do not wish to be recognized as a protectionist worrying about import competition, what could be better than getting your competitors to raise *their* costs of production closer to your levels by getting them to accept your standards? In short, turn Tom Friedman on his head: make the world flat when it is not. Level the playing field. Call it "fair trade." Pretend you are doing it for *their* workers, not yours, that you are being truly altruistic, and that your own self-interest is not the driving force behind those demands.

Obama has bought into the above because the Democratic Party has bought into it, and the party has bought into it because the labor unions bought the Democratic Party off at election time. Not surprisingly, the big, democratic countries such as Brazil and India see through this self-serving nonsense; when Howard Dean raised that demand at Davos this year, he was chewed out by Foreign Minister Celso Emorim of Brazil, as he deserved to be.

The sad part of the story is that there is no compelling evidence that trade with the poor countries is a significant factor in the workers' predicament and plenty of argumentation and evidence on the other side. So the Democrats' position on this issue is not merely protectionist in the sense of export protectionism but also based on a faulty empirical analysis. The sooner President Obama abandons that sanctimonious approach to the issue, which does him no credit, the better.

Instead he needs to use his intellectual ability and his political skills to steer the Democrats away from this *external* scapegoating of the issue of workers' wages and resulting obsession with labor and domestic environmental standards in trade treaties and institutions and focus instead on appropriate *domestic* institutional measures to expand union membership, and other related measures, to address the problem.

B. Foreign Investment. Three popular measures on direct foreign investment need to be distinguished, of which one is not protectionist:

1. Eliminate the incentive to go out. Presidential candidate Obama did claim during the campaign that he would remove any bias in U.S. tax law that encouraged U.S. firms to produce abroad rather than at home. (In his State of the Union address on February 25, he restated his disapproval of this bias, in, disappointingly, the only policy statement on the growing protectionism in his splendid speech.) Eliminating such a bias in our tax code is surely all right because no economist would be in favor of discriminatory taxation that distorts the choice of investment location.

2. Create incentives to invest at home rather than abroad. One should not discriminate by favoring the location of firms at home rather than abroad, for that would also be a distortion. Unfortunately, excoriating U.S. firms that invested abroad, especially when they closed down a plant in Nantucket and opened up one instead in Nairobi, was what Senator John Kerry did during his presidential campaign, calling such firms Benedict Arnolds. (Not having grown up in the United States, I thought that Benedict Arnold must be an obscure English poet, a distant cousin of Matthew Arnold, whom Senator Kerry had come across when he was at Yale because, unlike President George W. Bush, he must have been attending classes and getting good grades. But I was wrong on both counts. It turns out that Senator Kerry's grades were worse than those of President Bush. Besides, as every American schoolchild knows, Benedict Arnold was America's worst traitor. So Senator Kerry was calling such firms traitors.) The epithet was, in fact, applied increasingly to firms that simply bought online services and imported components from abroad, rather than just to those who folded operations at home and started them up abroad.

3. Sarkozy: Asking French firms to come home. President Sarkozy took the matter to its absurd extreme when he claimed that French firms already producing abroad (except when producing for the foreign host countries) should come home.

C. Hiring and Firing Immigrants. The proposed, and sometimes implemented, measures here include restrictions on hiring and encouraging the firing of foreigners: what might be described as admonitions, and occasional legislation, to hire citizens first and fire them last. With illegals, this has implied intensified enforcement and deportations in the United States. With legals, such as those brought in temporarily under H1 (b) visas, legislation requires tighter restrictions than before to ensure that no visa is issued if native workers have been laid off. Prime Minister Gordon Brown has faced pressures from British workers for such near-xenophobic measures.

Concluding Remarks

This sketch of the pressures building up to depart from openness in crisis indicates why President Obama's missing eloquence on openness to date is a matter of the utmost regret. Will he surprise us?

Contributors

Terry L. Anderson is the John and Jean De Nault Senior Fellow at the Hoover Institution and the executive director of PERC—the Property and Environment Research Center—a think tank in Bozeman, Montana, that focuses on market solutions to environmental problems. His research helped launch the idea of free market environmentalism and has prompted public debate over the proper role of government in managing natural resources. Anderson is the cochair of Hoover's Task Force on Property Rights, Freedom, and Prosperity.

Jagdish Bhagwati is a professor of economics and law at Columbia University and a senior fellow at the Council on Foreign Relations. Widely regarded as the leading scholar of international trade policy today, he has been honored with six festschrifts and many prizes and honorary degrees. He has also written frequently for leading newspapers and magazines, including the *Financial Times*, the *Wall Street Journal*, *Foreign Affairs,* and the *New Republic*. He has also been economic policy adviser to the director general of GATT, external policy adviser to the WTO, and economic policy adviser to the UN on globalization.

Charles W. Calomiris is the Henry Kaufman Professor of Financial Institutions at the Columbia University Graduate School of Business and a professor at Columbia's School of International and Public Affairs. Calomiris codirects the Project on Financial Deregulation at the American Enterprise Institute, where he is a visiting scholar. He is a member of the Shadow Financial Regulatory Committee and the Financial Economists Roundtable and a research associate of the National Bureau of Economic Research. Calomiris is a member of Hoover's Task Force on Property Rights, Freedom, and Prosperity.

Richard A. Epstein is the Peter and Kirsten Bedford Senior Fellow at Hoover. He also holds an endowed professorship at the University of Chicago Law School, where he directs the Law and Economics Program. As of 2007, he also became a visiting professor at New York University Law School. His areas of expertise include constitutional law, intellectual property, and property rights. His latest books are *Supreme Neglect: How to Revive the Constitutional Protection for Private Property,* (Oxford) and *The Case against the Employee Free Choice Act* (Hoover Press). He has been a member of the American Academy of Arts and Sciences since 1985. Epstein is a member of Hoover's Task Force on Property Rights, Freedom, and Prosperity.

Stephen H. Haber is the Peter and Helen Bing Senior Fellow at the Hoover Institution. He is also the A. A. and Jeanne Welch Milligan Professor in the School of Humanities and Sciences at Stanford, where he is a professor of political science, professor of history, and professor of economics (by courtesy). In addition, Haber is a senior fellow of the Stanford Institute for Economic Policy Research and a research economist at the National Bureau of Economic Research. He has consulted for the World Bank and the International Monetary Fund. His research focuses on the impact of fundamental political institutions on economic regulation and property rights systems. Much of his work has focused on Latin America, although he has also written on Africa, the Middle East, and the United States. Haber is a member of Hoover's Task Force on Property Rights, Freedom, and Prosperity.

Kevin A. Hassett is the director of economic policy studies and a senior fellow at the American Enterprise Institute (AEI). Before joining AEI, Hassett was a senior economist at the Board of Governors of the Federal Reserve System and an associate professor of economics and finance at the Graduate School of Business of Columbia University, as well as a policy consultant to the Treasury Department during the George H. W. Bush and Clinton administrations. He served as an economic adviser to the George W. Bush 2004 presidential campaign and as Senator McCain's chief economic adviser during the 2000 presidential primaries. He also served as a senior economic adviser to the McCain 2008 presidential campaign. Hassett writes a weekly column for Bloomberg.

James Huffman is the Erskine Wood Sr. Professor of Law at Lewis and Clark Law School in Oregon. He served as dean of the law school from 1993 to 2006. Huffman serves on the boards of the National Crime Victims Law Institute, the Foundation for Research on Economics and the Environment, the Classroom Law Project, and the Rocky Mountain Mineral Law Foundation. He is a member and former chair of the Executive Committee of the Environment and Property Rights Practice Group of the Federalist Society. His research interests include natural resource, property, environmental, and constitutional law. Huffman is a member of Hoover's Task Force on Property Rights, Freedom, and Prosperity.

F. Scott Kieff is a senior fellow at the Hoover Institution. He is also a professor at the Washington University School of Law and professor by courtesy at the Washington University School of Medicine's Department of Neurosurgery. He joined the Washington University faculty in 2001, after transitioning from his practice as a trial and intellectual property lawyer by serving as a visiting assistant professor at the University of Chicago Law School and Northwestern University School of Law. A former Hoover national fellow, he focuses on property rights in intangible assets, including finance and intellectual property, and he directs the Hoover Project on Commercializing Innovation. He is a member of Hoover's Task Force on Property Rights, Freedom, and Prosperity.

Gary D. Libecap is the Sherm and Marge Telleen Research Fellow at the Hoover Institution, the Bren Professor of Corporate Environmental Policy at the Donald R. Bren School of Environmental Science and Management, and an economics professor at the University of California, Santa Barbara. An expert on natural resource and environmental economics, he specializes in property rights and markets. His current research examines the legal and regulatory transaction costs of water marketing in the western United States. He is the cochair of Hoover's Task Force on Property Rights, Freedom, and Prosperity.

Henry E. Smith is a professor of law at Harvard Law School, where he directs the Project on the Foundations of Private Law. He teaches in the areas of property, intellectual property, natural resources, remedies, and taxation. He clerked for the Honorable Ralph K. Winter, U.S. Court of Appeals for the Second Circuit; has taught at the Northwestern University School of Law; and was the Fred A. Johnston Professor of Property and Environmental Law at Yale Law School. He has written primarily on the law and economics of property and intellectual property. Smith is a member of Hoover's Task Force on Property Rights, Freedom, and Prosperity.

Richard Sousa is senior associate director, director of the library and archives, and a research fellow at the Hoover Institution. An economist specializing in human capital, discrimination, labor economics, and K–12 education, he coauthored *School Figures: A Look at the Details behind the Debate* (2003), and his op-eds have appeared in newspapers throughout the country. He was a senior economist at Welch Consulting and Unicon Research Corporation and worked at the RAND Corporation.

Index

patents *(continued)*
  denying, 57
  eBay case, 2006, 57, 68
  eliminating unworthy, 55
  enforcing, 62–63
  equitable test, 67–69
  equity in remedies and, 67–69
  history of, lessons from, 59–62
  improving, 62–69
  Johns Hopkins v CellPro case, 1997/
    1998, 65
  junk, 56
  Jurgensen case, 1949, 60
  Knorr case, 2004, 65
  KSR case, 2007, 57, 58
  litigation and, baseless, 56
  New Deal and, 59
  New York Times and, 56
  nonobviousness requirement of,
    58, 60
  opinion of counsel about, 65
  Picard case, 1942, 61
  politics and, 59
  prior art and, 58
  problems with, 56
  Quanta case, 2008, 57
  reform, 55, 57–59
  Safety Car Heating & Lighting case,
    1946, 60
  social value of, 62
  specialization function of, 56
  symmetric fee shifting for, 66–67
  synergism test, 60, 61
  tangible property and, 67
  tightening standard for, 57
  trolls, 55, 56
  United States Supreme Court and,
    57
  validity of, 59–60, 64–65, 70

  Wall Street Journal and, 56
  weak, 56
Paul Wellstone Mental Health and
  Addiction Equity Act of 2008,
  114–15, 117
Paulson, Henry, 4, 6, 30
PD. *See* probability of default
Peri, Giovanni, 141
Peterson Institute, 77
Picard case, 1942, 61
political participation, 13
Poterba, James, 48
probability of default (PD), 28
property
  intellectual, 7
  law, 14
  patents and tangible, 67
  rights, ix, 1, 79
protectionism. *See* openness
Proxmire, William, 126

Quanta case, 2008, 57

rating agencies, 18, 22, 31
  avoiding grade inflation, 27–28
  buy side paying for, 27
  micromanaging, 27–28
  numbers and, 28
  for regulatory purposes, 22
  reliability of, 27
Reagan, Ronald, 61
real estate, 6
Recovery Zone Bonds, 42
regrowth, stimulating, 6–9
regulation, 18
  of banks, 21, 29, 31
  compartmentalized, 29–30
  competition for, 29
  complexity of, 24–25